Ce

Christianity
and the First
Christian Kings
in Britain

From St. Patrick and St. Columba,
to King Ethelbert and King Alfred

Paul Backholer

Celtic Christianity and the First Christian
Kings in Britain: From St. Patrick and St. Columba,
to King Ethelbert and King Alfred.

Scripture quotations are taken from:
- NKJV – The New King James Version. Published by Thomas Nelson, Inc. Copyright © 1982 by Thomas Nelson, Inc. Used by permission. All rights reserved.
- NIV – The New International Version®. NIV®. Copyright © 1973, 1978, 1984 by International Bible Society. Used by permission of Zondervan. All rights reserved.
- AV – Authorised Version / King James Version.

ISBN 978-1-907066-47-4
British Library Cataloguing In Publication Data.
A Record of this Publication is available
from the British Library.
First published in 2015 by ByFaith Media.
Second edition © 2016.
Third edition © 2017.
This book is also available as an ebook.

– Jesus Christ is Lord –

'They stayed there a long time, speaking boldly in the Lord, who was bearing witness to the word of His grace, granting signs and wonders to be done by their hands' (Acts 14:3).

"Go into all the world and preach the gospel to every creature. He who believes and is baptised will be saved; but he who does not believe will be condemned.

"And these signs will follow those who believe: In My name they will cast out demons; they will speak with new tongues; they will take up serpents; and if they drink anything deadly, it will by no means hurt them; they will lay hands on the sick, and they will recover" (Mark 16:15-18).

Contents

Christ with me, Christ before me,

Christ behind me, Christ within me,

Christ beneath me, Christ above me,

Christ at my right, Christ at my left,

Christ when I lie down, Christ when I rest,

Christ in the quiet, Christ when I arise,

Christ in the heart of all who thinks of me,

Christ in the mouth of all who speaks to me.

- Saint Patrick

Introduction

A Beautiful Revelation of God

Celtic Christianity defined the expression of faith in Ireland, Scotland, England and Wales for centuries. Its influence lasted in part, for up to seven hundred years. In fact, these believers preserved Christianity in Britain, and they pioneered the expansion of the Christian faith to Ireland and into parts of Europe.

Celtic Christians were the indigenous Christians of the British Isles, who emerged out of Roman culture after the fall of Roman rule in Britain. They created many unique Christian communities and expressions of the faith.

Celtic believers in Jesus Christ shared a profound belief in signs and wonders taking place in the world, with solid doctrine straight from Scripture guiding the way. They embraced the promise of Jesus that, "These signs shall follow those who believe" (Mark 16:17), and like Peter, believed God gives Holy Spirit inspired visions, dreams, prophecies and speaks through His creation to point to Jesus Christ (Acts 2:14-21, Romans 1:20, 2 Peter 3:4).

Whilst the pagans had abolished civilisation in parts of Europe after the fall of the Roman Empire, during the Celtic Golden Age in Britain and Ireland, Celtic Christian communities pioneered and produced some of the greatest masterpieces of art and literature in the world. The Dark Ages did not exist where Celtic Christianity thrived. Celtic believers also shared their faith, wisdom and technology with Europeans, as they took the gospel to the Germanic peoples who had yet to hear of Christ.

The Celtic expression of the Christian faith was one of sacrifice. In the manner of Jesus Christ and John the Baptist, many leading Celtic Christians withdrew into the wilderness and sought God, in austerity, until they received a beautiful revelation of the God of the Bible in their own hearts. They learnt to bring their bodies under subjection to Christ and this enabled their spirit to be in tune with God the Holy Spirit (1 Corinthians 9:27).

What took place in the Christian communities of Britain and Ireland was a unique revelation of God, based upon the Bible, which echoed the writings and experiences of the apostles and prophets within Scripture. These believers embraced the stillness of God, with a rejection of worldliness. They felt Christ speak to them through creation, whilst they cherished education, art, pioneered technology and cared for the poor.

The Celts, the native inhabitants of the British Isles, were at first pagans, but as Christianity arrived in Britain during the British Roman era, people began to respond to the message they heard. The faith began to spread amongst the Celts and when the Roman Empire collapsed in Britain, the independent Celtic witness sprung alive in ways which could never have been anticipated, flourishing in the fifth and sixth centuries. The Celtic Golden Age which began with the finished work of Patrick in Ireland lasted for at least two hundred and fifty years in the British Isles and beyond.

The death of Roman Britain enabled Celtic Christianity to come into full bloom. Into the void created by the loss of Roman rule, a unique British form of Christianity evolved, with links to the first generations of believers in Jesus Christ from the Middle East.

These Celtic Christians did indeed fellowship with and engaged with other believers in foreign lands. When the Roman Empire converted to Christianity and the Bishop of Rome identified himself as the Pope, in a new imperial brand of Christianity, some Middle Eastern followers of Jesus Christ fled to the deserts to avoid the corruption of power, politics and religion combined. The ascetic movement in Egypt seemed to have an impact abroad and some Celtic Christians followed the example of the Egyptian Christians to flee corrupting alliances, to meet with God in the hills and valleys.

Whilst the new brand of 'Roman Catholic' faith was to be imperial in nature and ambition, much like the Roman Empire, British Celtic Christianity flourished and spread because it inspired people to follow the same paths as Christ in humility and sacrifice.

For Celtic Christians, the inner life of Christ in them and the reality of eternal life were more important than any temporal influence. Consequently, the disciples of Jesus Christ in Britain and Ireland nurtured their prayer lives and taught that prayer should be as natural as breathing. They cherished fellowship with God and affirmed the equality and priesthood of all believers.

For these British followers of Jesus Christ, Peter was a simple fisherman called and chosen by God to preach Christ's gospel. The concept of Peter as a Pope had not yet been invented. But like Peter, the Celtic Christians lived simple lives and serve God and became God's holy priests. 'You are a chosen generation, a royal priesthood, a holy nation, His own special people, that you may proclaim the praises of Him who called you out of darkness into His marvellous light' (1 Peter 2:9).

The legacy left behind by this pioneering age of faith in and around the British Isles was one of revolutionary and extreme sacrificial discipleship, which can be rewarded by an intimate relationship with Christ, by the Holy Spirit (Romans 8:26). From Celtic centres of communal faith was preached a message of peace in Christ, justice and equality for all, including slaves. For the Celts, faith in God could never be excluded from any area of life, and Christ was to be honoured the same in work, as well as in prayer, with no divide between the secular and sacred.

Celtic Christians had a large missionary heart. Burning in their souls was the missionary zeal to take the message of Jesus Christ to those who had never heard. First the gospel went from Roman Britain to Ireland, as the Spirit of God sent Patrick to that nation. Then Patrick's disciples spread the faith far into Scotland, and south into England, after the pagan invasions which had decimated Christianity in the land of the Anglo-Saxons.

Missionaries from Rome to Britain claimed the imperial power of the Pope to seek conversions, whilst Celtic missionaries confirmed God was working in and through them with signs and wonders. The weakness of the

Celtic Christian approach was that heresy could develop unchecked in their non-hierarchical structure of Church leadership. Meanwhile, its strength was that in isolation on the fringes of the known world, Celtic followers of Jesus Christ were able to continue a culture of faith which was arguably closer to the early Church, than the institutionalised Roman faith that eventually replaced it.

For two and a half pioneering centuries the Celtic Golden Age shone and yet a political decision made by a king would finally end its influence, as Britain and later Ireland officially became Roman Catholic. If the spread of Celtic Christianity had continued in Britain and in parts of Europe, the Reformation beginning in 1517 may have never needed to take place.

It was the failure of Celtic Christians to become shrewd and political, which eventually led to their demise. They were unable to understand or appreciate the calculative political dealings which led to a king in Britain converting the nation to the Roman brand of faith. Nevertheless, their legacy of supernatural faith, grounded in the Bible, stands as a testimony to a true Golden Age of faith.

The Celts experienced Holy Spirit inspired miracles, visions and dreams, which was the demonstration of God's power in them, leading to the conversion of much of Ireland, Scotland, England and Wales. Nevertheless, in the limited writings they have left to us, we find a deep and unconditional commitment to Scripture for doctrine. They were not modern environmentalists or New Agers, but instead they sought New Testament Christianity.

Celtic Christians wanted to be like Jesus Christ and His disciples. The apostles of Jesus paid a high price to walk closely with their God, by the power of the Holy Spirit, and many Celtic Christians followed the same path of sacrificial faith. They believed that as long as the full price of discipleship was paid, they could discover an astonishing closeness with God. They embraced the mysterious revelation of God to them in the 'thin places,' but this was not some vague spirituality. Celtic Christianity was exactly that – Christianity, set and expressed in a Celtic culture which was being redeemed.

Whilst embracing personal revelation for themselves from God, they accepted that God has already revealed Himself to the world, and His testimony has been written down, once and for all time in Scripture (2 Timothy 3:16). Nonetheless, God is not to be found in ritual, but rather in personal revelation which drives people to Scripture.

Throughout its varied history, it could be argued that Celtic Christianity went through three major stages of development. The following is a simplified version of these stages:

At first Celtic Christianity was just another reflection of Christianity within Roman Britain. This was a time of tiny beginnings, as Christianity and Celtic culture fused, within the context of the dominant influence of Roman culture. The foundations were being laid.

The second period began with the collapse of Roman rule in Britain from AD 407, and Celtic Christianity at first struggled to survive, and then thrived, leading to the two hundred and fifty year Celtic Golden Age of education and missions.

The third period began with the Synod of Whitby in AD 644, as the Roman Catholic brand of Christianity was forced upon the Celts, by a king who needed the international connections that being Catholic could bring. Following this development, the Celtic leaders began their slow two centuries withdrawal and loss of religious heritage, until there was little of their uniqueness left. What Rome failed to take, the Viking raiders finally destroyed, as they erased the last vestiges of the faith.

Throughout their seven centuries of potential influence, the Celtic expression of the Christian faith evolved and transmuted in many communities. Some of the Celtic leaders could be harsh in their devotion to an absolute sacrificial faith. In Wales, the Monastic Rule of St David insisted that monks had to plough the fields without animals, whilst only eating minimal bread and drinking water. In Ireland and England, some hermits would stand in the freezing sea for hours to pray, whilst others lived in tiny rock huts on isolated islands.

By studying information from the Celtic Christian age,

we can find eight principles which guided them, which may be a blessing to Christians today.

1. The most sacred treasures we have are the Gospels of our Lord Jesus Christ. All holy Scripture is to be read, studied, pondered, prayed-over, cherished, preserved, duplicated and passed to all generations (Psalm 119:105, 1 Timothy 4:15, 2 Timothy 3:16-17).

2. Sacrifice, austerity and simplicity. Christ was humble in spirit but rich in faith and hope, and we must follow His example of sacrificial faith. Worldliness (or consumerism today) can find no place in true disciples of Jesus Christ (Philippians 2:5-8, 17, 1 Peter 2:5).

3. The Infinite and Eternal Triune God can never be fully comprehended or explained by finite man. Only the Holy Spirit can reveal God to you and Christ in you (1 Corinthians 4:1, 1 Timothy 6:16).

4. Follow the Holy Spirit wherever He leads, whatever the cost, as did Patrick, and the Spirit of God will reveal Christ in you (John 15:16-17, 26-27, 1 John 3:24, 4:13).

5. The final command of Christ – to make disciples of all nations – is the reason the Church exists, and why we must remain on earth as strangers and pilgrims to be His witnesses. The gospel must be taken to the ends of the earth and all must have a chance to hear of Jesus' death and resurrection, with signs and wonders following, as a witness to God's power (Luke 24:46-48, Mark 16:15-20).

6. All are equal and one in Christ. There is no special class of priests who can mediate between God and man. All can embrace intimacy with God, through Jesus Christ (Galatians 3:28, 1 Timothy 2:5, 1 Peter 2:5, 9.)

7. God is ever present and we must abide in Him at all times and in all places. Every second of our lives, including as we work, is as sacred as our spiritual lives, because God is omnipresent (Psalm 139:7, Romans 14:8, Colossians 3:23, Philippians 4:13, 1 Peter 4:11).

8. God's creation is to be cherished, as part of His gift and revelation to us. It is not to be worshipped, because its purpose is to point us to God (Acts 17:28, Romans 1:20, Romans 8:21-22).

Chapter One

Celtic Faith

To appreciate what Celtic Christianity was and how it changed Britain and Ireland, we must first consider how Christianity came to Britain and how it spread.

In the first century 'Britain had its own set of religious icons: pagan gods of the earth and Roman gods of the sky. Into this superstitious and violent world came a modern, fashionable faith from the east: Christianity. We tend to associate the arrival of Christianity in Britain with the mission of Augustine in AD 597. But in fact Christianity arrived long before then, and in the first century, there wasn't an organised attempt to convert the British. It began as Roman artisans and traders arrived spreading the story of Jesus Christ in Britain. Unlike the many faiths of Rome, Christianity demanded exclusive allegiance from its followers. It was this pure devotion to one God, which rattled the Roman authorities and led to repeated persecutions of Christians. Christians were forced to meet and worship in secret.'[1]

Dr Robert Bedford explains, "History tells us that Christianity first arrived in Britain from the Mediterranean during the Roman occupation. It was an import, like the roads, army, drainage and everything else, and its focus was in the cities," like Verulamium, at St Albans, in Hertfordshire, "which was once the third largest city in Roman Britain."[2]

The native Christians of this age were cut-off from Rome and there was no official attempt to impose a religious system upon them; instead Roman citizens brought their Christian faith with them, and native Celts listened to the message and responded, to join Roman citizens in their new faith in Jesus Christ.

Christianity spread in Britain and the Church Father Tertullian (160-225) of Carthage, Tunisia, states that

Christianity greatly impacted Britain, and some areas inaccessible to the Romans accepted Christianity: 'The haunts of the Britons, inaccessible to the Romans, but subjugated to Christ,' he declared.[3] Thus, according to Tertullian, Christianity spread further than the Roman occupation in Britain ever did, perhaps far into Scotland.

The Bishop of Caesarea and historian Eusebius (AD 260-340) believed some of the first generation of Christians, the converts of the first disciples, came to preach in Britain: 'To preach to all the name of Jesus, to teach about His marvellous deeds...and some have crossed the Ocean and reached the Isles of Britain.'[4]

The first Christians in Britain met in their homes to worship, as did the disciples of Jesus Christ, until toleration enabled wealthy Romans to set aside large rooms in their homes, to be dedicated for a permanent place of worship. In the British Museum resides one part of a Christian wall painting, showing men praying from Lullingstone, Kent, which was removed from a Roman villa. English heritage states: 'The evidence of the Christian house-church is a unique discovery for Roman Britain and the wall-paintings are of international importance...they provide some of the earliest evidence for Christianity in Britain.'[5]

Archaeological evidence also provides us with examples of Christian communities developing in the third and fourth centuries, with possible small timber churches at Lincoln and Silchester, and baptismal fonts have been discovered at Saxon Shore Fort in Richborough. By this time, ten percent of the Roman Empire had accepted Christianity, and even though we have no statistical data available for the province of Britannia, there is no reason to believe it had not achieved such importance in this land.[6]

Archaeological finds point to clear signs of the strength of Christianity among some of the middle and upper classes, who have left physical objects to study. In the British Museum, a lead tank from Icklingham provides us with firsthand data from a Christian community. The British Museum states: 'This lead tank is one of three found at Icklingham, where an early church and cemetery have been excavated. On the side of the tank in two places is the common Christian device of a Chi-Rho symbol, the first two letters of Christ's name in Greek. This is flanked by an alpha and omega, the first and last letters of the Greek alphabet, another symbol of Christ – 'I am Alpha and Omega, the first and the last' (Revelation 1:8).'[7]

The fact that Christianity was flourishing in Britain is further attested by the Christian silver plaque and gold disc from the Water Newton treasure, which the British Museum explains is: 'The earliest Christian silver yet found in the Roman Empire'[8] and it was found, having been used by Christians in Britain. In the find is a chalice, similar to ones later used in communion services. The British Museum states: 'Many of the objects in the hoard bear the monogram formed by the Greek letters chi (X) and rho (P), the first two letters of Christ's name, a symbol commonly used by early Christians. Two bowls and one plaque have longer inscriptions in Latin. One of these, on a bowl, can be translated as 'I, Publianus, honour your sacred shrine, trusting in you, O Lord.' Other inscriptions give the names of three female dedicators: Amcilla, Innocentia and Viventia, who must also have belonged to the congregation.'[9]

Throughout Britain, other ancient places of Christian worship have been found, including in Colchester and Poundbury. But we must remember that poorer Christians could not afford to leave any open legacy, so the true extent of the Church in Britain remains unknown. The fact that these Christians tended to meet in their homes makes it impossible to measure the size or scope of Christianity in Britain. Yet, when Christian leaders met in France, at the Council of Arles in 314, British Celtic Christianity was strong enough to send three bishops – Eborius of York, Restitutus of London and Adelphius, possibly a bishop of Lincoln. As we have already explained, Christians made up about ten percent of the Roman Empire by this time, so the numbers of believers in Britain could have been substantial.[10]

Theological disputes were common in this age and Britain was engaging with and being rebuked by other believers. In an open letter to many nations defending the faith, Hilary, the Bishop of Poitiers (300-368) says, 'To the bishops of the provinces of Britain...the whole faith is summed up and secured in this, the Trinity must always be preserved, as we read in the gospel, "Go ye and baptise all nations in the name of the Father, and of the Son, and of the Holy Ghost." '[11]

"The British Isles, which are beyond the sea and which lie in the ocean, have received the virtue of the Word," exclaimed John Chrysostom (347-407), the Bishop of Constantinople in 402. 'Churches are there founded and altars erected. Though you should go to the ocean, to the British Isles, there you will hear all men everywhere discoursing matters out of the Scriptures, with a different voice indeed, but not another faith, with a different tongue but the same judgment."[12]

Before Christianity was legalised in the Roman Empire, the majority of believers still clung to New Testament Christianity and many were martyred for their faith in Christ, including in Britain. Their commitment to Christ, unto death, seems to have inspired many of the pagans to convert.

Sometime during the third or fourth century, a Christian called Alban became venerated as the first official English martyr, with many others following. In the ancient book *On the Ruin and Conquest of Britain* by Gildas the Wise (500-570), he writes how the Church in Britain survived the Diocletian persecution: 'God, therefore, who wishes all men to be saved and who calls sinners no less than those who think themselves righteous, magnified His mercy towards us, and as we know, during the above named persecution, that Britain might not totally be enveloped in the dark shades of night, He, of His own free gift, kindled up among us bright luminaries of holy martyrs...such were Saint Alban of Verulamium, Aaron and Julius, citizens of the City of the Legions, and the rest, of both sexes, who in different places stood their ground in the Christian contest.'[13] This book is one of the most significant sources of history of ancient Britain, as it is the only one written by a near contemporary of the age.

To the Romans, Britain and Ireland symbolised the end of the known world, because to the west of Cornwall, Scotland or Ireland lay an impassable sea, where the sun set. All who reached Britain touched the mysterious lands of the north west, and many came. There are several myths and legends of biblical characters crossing the English Channel, such as the visit of Joseph of Arimathea in AD 37, which unsubstantiated, cannot provide us with any factual basis to claim any historical reliability. In none of the earliest references to Christianity's arrival in Britain is Joseph of Arimathea mentioned,[14] and these legends were most probably invented by monks in the Middle Ages seeking pilgrims.

Before there was any organised attempt to bring Christianity to the nation, God in His great sovereignty orchestrated the spread of the gospel, and by the fourth and fifth centuries, Christianity thrived. Enough evidence exists to prove that a strong Christian Church was unmistakably evident in Britain, amidst a cloud of paganism. These first believers in Britain provide us with a close link to Jesus and the apostles.

The father of English history, the Venerable Bede (673-735), in his chronicles of the *Ecclesiastical History of the English People* provides us with further details of Christianity in Britain, from its earliest days, but with the collapse of Roman rule in Britain between AD 407-410, the future became uncertain.

Chapter Two

Invasion and Hope

A terrible period for Celtic Christianity emerged with the arrival of a few ships of heavily armed warriors, who landed on England's east coast, beginning in the mid-fifth century. These pagan warrior tribes were the Angles, Saxons, Jutes and Frisians. These Germanic tribes overran England and decapitated the government, filling the power-vacuum left in the province of Britannia after the Roman Empire withdrew between AD 407-410, and they also brought their horrendous pagan gods.

In a dramatic turn of events, the Roman life of villas, towns, international trade, luxury, law and order collapsed. The only part of life under Roman occupation which survived was Christianity. These Celtic Christians no longer had any form of protection and the leadership of the indigenous people of Britain fled west out of the way of the pagan invaders. As these Germanic invaders slashed and burned villages, so the great Celtic exodus began. Many Celtic Christians withdrew into the west of southern Scotland, northern England, west Cornwall, Wales and some to Ireland. Others fled into Europe, taking their faith with them as they sought a peaceful society, free from the pagan invaders.

As the Germanic pagans ravished town after town in England, literacy, technology, towns and Christianity itself disappeared, to be replaced with pagan warlike gods, chaos and illiteracy. The Brittonic languages which were once spoken in the land, withdrew into the Celtic strongholds of west Britain, especially Wales. Of these original languages spoken by Britons when the Romans ruled, Welsh is a direct descendant. As a Bible College student I studied in Wales on a campus called 'Derwen Fawr' which has Brittonic origins, as does, albeit indirectly, London, Aberdeen, York, Dorchester, Dover,

Colchester and the rivers Avon, Chew and Frome.

One myth of the Germanic invasions is that they flooded the nation in such large numbers, that they overwhelmed the native inhabitants and forced them all to flee. "The Anglo-Saxon chronicle tells us that they were coming over in really quite small numbers of people – two or three long boats," explains the archaeologist Dr Neil Faulkner. "You can get about thirty, forty, fifty people into a long boat. That means it's actually quite a small number of warriors who are coming in."[1]

An exodus of Celtic leaders and Christians pioneers certainly took place into the west of England, Wales, Cornwall, Ireland and Scotland, but the Anglo-Saxon invaders simply became the foreign rulers of the British inhabitants who could not flee. Those who remained chose to adopt Anglo-Saxon culture and beliefs to be accepted by their new rulers. They became culturally Anglo-Saxon and the nationality we now identify as 'English,' is a derivative of 'Anglo.' Nevertheless, the main body of people in England were still natives, Celts if you like, and this has been proved by DNA analysis of the descendants of the traditional inhabitants of Britain.

Dr Stephen Oppenheimer, an expert in genetic science analysis, has methodically examined the extensive studies of the DNA of the British and concludes, "The Anglo-Saxon contribution, in my analysis, is only five percent for the whole of England. The English are much closer to the Welsh, the Irish, the Cornish and the Scottish than they are to any continental population. This idea of the English coming in as a race – or the Anglo-Saxons coming in as a race – really just doesn't hold up in the genetic view."[2]

Therefore, the majority of the traditional inhabitants of Britain continue to be the descendants of the Britons who were living in the land when Rome invaded. Future intermarriages between the descendants of these Britons and Anglo-Saxons, Vikings, Normans and other invaders, though culturally significant, still remain relatively minor in the DNA analysis. Dr Neil Faulkner concludes, "So most of the people that we think of as

Anglo-Saxon are actually British people who've been integrated into Anglo-Saxon society."[3]

Nevertheless, the pagans took over England and reversed all the progress which had been made by the Roman Empire.[4] The great Roman cities and centres with a vibrant Christian witness died a sudden death and Christianity was killed-off wherever the pagans arrived. "Only in the West and in Ireland did Christianity remain a real force," explains Dr Robert Bedford. "Ireland had never been part of the Roman Empire, but just as the Empire was collapsing, Christian missionaries arrived under the leadership of Saint Patrick and here Christianity took a radically different form. It was devoted to austerity and mysticism."[5]

It's not entirely clear what reasons the Celtic Christians gave for why God allowed the collapse of Roman rule in the province of Britannica, and the subsequent invasion of the pagans, leading to the decimation of Christianity. In the case of the city of Rome and its Empire, St Augustine of Hippo (354-430) argues in his book *The City of God Against the Pagans* that followers of Jesus Christ are strangers and pilgrims on earth, as Scripture states. As this is the case, Christians must seek the heavenly city of God, instead of putting their trust in earthly powers, like Rome (Hebrews 11:13). But what did the Celtic Christians in Britain think about their situation? Perhaps there is a case to be made that Celtic Christians in Britain believed the legalisation of Christianity in the Roman Empire had made becoming a follower of Jesus too comfortable and worldly?

Gold and silver objects used in worship, now safe in museums, may have served posterity well by surviving as a testimony to their faith, but what about Jesus' teaching about riches and James' warning against them in James 5:1-6? Jesus said, "Do not lay up for yourselves treasures on earth, where moth and rust destroy and where thieves break in and steal; but lay up for yourselves treasures in heaven, where neither moth nor rust destroys and where thieves do not break in and steal. For where your treasure is, there your heart will be also" (Matthew 6:19-21).

Jesus Christ never gave a command to build churches like palaces, nor did He ask for gold and silver objects to be made for use in worship. This is legacy of the Roman Empire and its first Christian Emperor, Constantine the Great (272-337), beginning with his churches in Rome. The Roman Empire loved gold and silver, but many of the prophets of the Old Testament shunned the world and its wealth. John the Baptist, Jesus Christ and His apostles spent time in the deserts seeking God, and they were often poor or homeless (1 Corinthians 4:11). Jesus said, "Foxes have holes and birds of the air have nests, but the Son of Man has nowhere to lay His head" (Luke 9:58). The example of Jesus Christ was one of sacrifice, austerity, death to self and helping those in need (Matthew 6:3-4).

So did Christianity in Britain become worldly when it was legalised under Roman rule, or was the Germanic invasions just one of those terrible things which happen? According to the Old Testament, God allowed the Kingdoms of Israel and Judah to fall into the hands of ungodly foreign powers, because they had not been faithful to God's will and this teaching may have made an impact on the Celtic Christians. The word 'because' is found 1,138 in the King James Bible from the year 1611, and in the biblical books of Kings, Chronicles, Jeremiah and other prophetic books, God tells His people they were to be exiled, 'Because...'

What is certain is that Celtic Christianity in Ireland and western Britain was to be vastly different from the faith of many Popes, who embraced the legacy of the golden churches of Constantine's Rome. The Celtic believers were committed to austerity and the supernatural manifestation of God's power. They spent time outside in nature, following the example of John the Baptist and Jesus, seeking God in prayer, and bringing their physical bodies into subjection to their spirit. 'Of whom the world was not worthy. They wandered in deserts and mountains, in dens and caves of the earth' (Hebrews 11:38).

As we have identified, Christianity remained strong in Cornwall, Wales, west England and the west of southern Scotland, but England's first historian, the Venerable Bede, was deeply troubled that these Celtic Christians never gained the courage to return east into the newly pagan regions of England to share the gospel with the invaders, their subjects and their descendants. Instead Christianity was first sent into Ireland, before it could flourish and bounce back into Britain, via Scotland and south into England.

Chapter Three

Patrick and Ireland

The most important figure in the development of this age of Celtic Christianity was the missionary Patrick, a fifth century Romano-British man, the son of a follower of Jesus Christ. Born somewhere in England, young Patrick was at best, a nominal Christian when he was captured by pirates around AD 400 and was taken to Ireland to be sold as a slave. Whilst tending sheep in his enslavement, he re-committed himself to Jesus Christ and spent hours in prayer in the hills.

Patrick believed there was a reason and meaning for all the events which happened to him and he tells us in his own words, the reasons for his captivity: 'I was then about sixteen years of age. I did not know the true God. I was taken into captivity to Ireland with many thousands of people, and deservedly so, because we turned away from God, and did not keep His commandments, and did not obey our ministers, who used to remind us of our salvation. And the Lord brought over us the wrath of His anger and scattered us among many nations, even unto the utmost part of the earth, where now my littleness is placed among strangers. And there the Lord opened the sense of my unbelief that I might at last remember my sins and be converted with all my heart to the Lord my God, who had regard for my abjection, and mercy on my youth and ignorance, and watched over me before I knew Him, and before I was able to distinguish between good and evil, and guarded me and comforted me as would a father his son.'[1]

Patrick spent six years as a slave and he tells us, 'I prayed a hundred times in the day and almost as many at night,' and one night as he sought God, he heard God's voice saying, "It is well that you fast. Soon you will go to your own country," and after a short while, "See, your ship is ready." Patrick escaped slavery and made it across the Irish Sea to England.

It's important to separate the real human being Patrick, from the legends, myths and perceptions that have been built around him. He was not trained and sent out due to the legacy of Emperor Constantine's Church and he declared: 'I have not studied like the others.' Instead Patrick had a personal relationship with God, based upon Divine revelation from the Holy Spirit and complete submission to the authority and doctrines of Scripture. In his writings, Patrick shows a thorough knowledge of the doctrines of the apostles in the New Testament. He wrote Jesus 'was made Man, and, having defeated death, was received into heaven by the Father; and He hath given Him all power over all names in heaven, on earth, and under the earth, and every tongue shall confess to Him that Jesus Christ is Lord.'[2]

After settling back into life as a freeman in England, Patrick received a dream from God which asked of him, the very thing he never wanted to do – return to Ireland. 'There I saw in the night the vision of a man, whose name was Victoricus, coming as it were from Ireland, with countless letters. And he gave me one of them, and I read the opening words of the letter, which were, "The voice of the Irish." I read the beginning of the letter, I thought that at the same moment I heard their voice... and thus did they cry out as with one mouth, "We ask thee, boy, come and walk among us once more." And I was quite broken in heart and could read no further, and so I woke up. Thanks be to God, after many years the Lord gave to them according to their cry. And another night... they called me... except that at the end of the prayer He spoke thus, "He that has laid down His life for thee, it is He that speaketh in thee," and so I awoke full of joy.'[3]

Patrick's faith was wholeheartedly committed to New Testament Christianity, which included a belief in dreams and visions from God, grounded in the veracity of Scripture (Acts 2:17, 10:9-16, 16:19). Patrick heard the voice of Jesus and he also learnt to become sensitive to the Holy Spirit, just like the apostles: 'As they ministered to the Lord and fasted, the Holy Spirit said, "Now separate to Me Barnabas and Saul for the work to which I have called them" ' (Acts 13:2). Patrick testifies: 'I saw Him praying in me and I was as it were within my body, and I heard Him above me, that is, over the inward man and there He prayed mightily with groanings. And all the time I was astonished, and wondered and thought with myself who it could be that prayed in me. But at the end of the prayer He spoke, saying that He was the Spirit; and so I woke up, and remembered the Apostle saying: 'The Spirit helpeth the infirmities of our prayer. For we know not what we should pray for as we ought; but the Spirit Himself asketh for us with unspeakable groanings, which cannot be expressed in words' (Romans 8:26-27); and again: 'The Lord our advocate asketh for us' '[4] (1 John 2).

Patrick followed the command of God and began his mission to take the Christian faith to the ends of the known earth, as far west as Christianity had ever gone. He added, 'I, however ignorant as I was, in the last days dared to undertake such a holy and wonderful work, thus imitating somehow those who, as the Lord once foretold, would preach His gospel for a testimony to all nations before the end of the world.'[5]

"When he made landfall in the north of Ireland, he brought with him the promise of a new civilisation, rooted in Christianity," explains the historian Dan Snow. "But he was entering a land where paganism ran deep. Ireland was a place of sacred trees, woods and lakes, presided over by druids, combining the roles of priest, wise man and ritual executioner. There's was a religion of animal and human sacrifice, of blood on altars and entrails that were used to tell the future. The druid religion had once extended right across Western Europe. The Romans were so disturbed by it they made it illegal on pain of death, but Rome's authority had never extended into Ireland and here it had continued to flourish."[6]

Monsignor Raymond Murray, parish priest of Cookstown in Northern Ireland explains, "Part of the pagan worship of fall to spring, from the beginning of the summer, was that a fire was lit, and first of all, the fire on the hill of Tara and no other lights at all in Ireland. This monastery on the hill of Slane is where Patrick – in direct defiance of the high King of Tara – lit a forbidden fire."[7]

Patrick plunged a spiritual dagger into the heart of paganism in Ireland and he was dragged before the king, with the expectation of being executed. Being asked to explain himself, Patrick was able to convince the king that the Christian God was more powerful than any of the gods the king was serving, and Christianity was adopted and flourished.

In 432, Patrick built the first church in Ireland, on the site of the present day St. Patrick's Memorial Church, in Saul. Thousands were baptised and hundreds of churches were planted across Ireland. Patrick, having been led by the Holy Spirit to Ireland, to glorify Jesus Christ, decided to follow a completely different direction from the bishops of Rome, and when the rich offered him gifts, he refused them. He was worried by this, confessing, 'I offended the donors...but, guided by God...I came to the people of Ireland to preach the gospel...For I am very much God's debtor.' He was not always welcome and had to 'suffer insult from the unbelievers.'[8]

Monasteries like the one at Labbamolaga "began to appear across Ireland soon after Patrick's missions of 432," explains the historian Dr Janina Ramirez, "because they were disconnected from mainland Christian Europe, in particular Rome and the Papacy, the monasteries that developed across Celtic lands were rather different to those on the Continent. Monasticism on the Continent evolved as part of the existing Roman Church hierarchy, but the Romans hadn't come to Ireland."[9]

Patrick's Celtic Christianity emphasised personal sacrifice, love for God, openness to the Holy Spirit and the apostles' conviction that believers should live as slaves of Jesus Christ. Patrick saw his life's mission was to do all to fulfil the command of Christ. He wrote: 'To Thee the Gentiles shall come from the ends of the earth and shall say, "How false are the idols that our fathers got for themselves and there is no profit in them;" and again, "I have set Thee as a light among the Gentiles, that Thou mayest be for salvation unto the utmost part of the earth." And there I wish to wait for His promise who surely never deceives, as He promises in the gospel.'

Patrick was consumed with Christ's Great Commission, that every creature must be reached with the gospel (Mark 16:15-18), and he copied out all the Scriptures concerning Jesus' command to take His gospel to the ends of the earth. He wrote: 'Go therefore now, teach all nations, baptising them in the name of the Father and the Son, and the Holy Spirit, teaching them to observe all things...I will pour out of My Spirit upon all flesh; and your sons and your daughters shall prophesy, and your young men shall see visions, and your old men shall dream dreams.' Thus, 'it came to pass in Ireland that those who never had a knowledge of God, but until now always worshipped idols and things impure, have now been made a people of the Lord, and are called sons of God.'[10]

Patrick's was a pure ministry, motivated by God's Spirit and he was bold to challenge anyone to give evidence that he abused his authority. 'When I baptised so many thousands of people, did I perhaps expect from any of them as much as half a scruple? Tell me and I will restore it to you. Or when the Lord ordained clerics everywhere through my unworthy person and I conferred the ministry upon them free, if I asked any of them as much as the price of my shoes, speak against me and I will return it to you.'[11]

His faith was a stark contrast to the example which had been set in Rome. Former British Cabinet Minister and broadcaster Michael Portillo describes the influence of Constantine on the Church in Rome, "For centuries Christians had been persecuted, they'd been fed to lions, they'd been living underground in catacombs, they'd been worshipping in churches no bigger than a house, and then along comes Constantine and showers them with riches. Well, you're not going to say no, are you?

You're not going to look a gift-horse in the mouth. But if since the time of Christ you've been preaching blessed are the meek and blessed are the poor, and you inherit all this (the newly constructed golden churches of Rome), its bound to change you, isn't it?"[12]

Michael Portillo added, "The emperor showered Christians with wealth and built wondrous churches in Rome and Constantinople. Christianity moved overnight from being a minority movement of underdogs to being enthroned. Some commentators regard the change as disastrous, because Christ's revolutionary message that the meek would inherit the earth sits uncomfortably with the Church's wealth and power. On the other hand, had Christianity not become established throughout the Empire, would there have been so many converts across the centuries, each one representing, for believers, a soul saved?"[13]

Patrick, like the apostle Paul was bold enough to ask his converts if he had exploited any and invited them to come to him for recompense (2 Corinthians 7:2). By the end of his life he could testify: 'For Christ the Lord, too, was poor for our sakes; and I, unhappy wretch that I am, have no wealth even if I wished for it.'[14] Paul wrote: 'Nor did we eat anyone's bread free of charge, but worked with labour and toil night and day, that we might not be a burden to any of you, not because we do not have authority, but to make ourselves an example of how you should follow us' (2 Thessalonians 3:8-9).

Celtic Christianity, as Patrick's life proves, initially remained true to New Testament Christianity and it was also alive in the west of Britain. However, it was to be the followers of Patrick's example, who would bring Christianity back to the pagan areas of England and stretch far into uncharted areas of Scotland.

As for Patrick, he wanted to return to Britain, but he felt no liberty in the Holy Spirit: 'Wherefore, then, even if I wished to leave them and go to Britain, and how I would have loved to go to my country and my parents...God knows it, I much desired it; but I am bound by the Spirit, who gives evidence against me if I do this, telling me that

I shall be guilty. I am afraid of losing the labour which I have begun, nay, not I, but Christ the Lord who bade me come here and stay with them for the rest of my life.'[15]

Patrick was an independent missionary to Ireland, resisted by men, but sent by a direct revelation of the Lord Jesus Christ, by the leading of the Holy Spirit, to risk his life so pagans could receive eternal life. His own writings testify that he walked closely with God and like the apostles of Jesus, developed a deep sensitivity to the guidance of God's Holy Spirit. In subsequent generations his writings would be ignored, as he was recast into a new religious image, to fit with the ever changing times; but when we return to his testimony, what we find is New Testament Christianity.

Chapter Four

The Celtic Light in Ireland, Scotland, England and Wales

Patrick, as a young man born and raised in Britain, accepted the seeds of New Testament Christianity from his family, which they received from believers who travelled along the Roman roads. After taking his faith seriously, he was sent by God as a missionary to Ireland and the revolution which he sparked there, changed Ireland from a pagan backwater to the beating heart of a spiritual, technological and missionary minded nation. It was a spiritual revolution, just as influential as the Industrial Revolution.

Patrick preached in a nation which had never been occupied by the Romans, and when he arrived it had no roads, no towns, no stone buildings and no Christianity; but with his message of faith a transformation took place. Within fifty years of his first sermon, Ireland became a centre of civilisation, with economic dynamism, modernity, language, literacy and education, centred on the monasteries which were quickly erected.

"Nowadays books and libraries are so much part of our culture that it's impossible to imagine a time without them," said the historian Dan Snow. "But the sixth century was just such a time. Of course there would have been books under the Romans, in fact there were dozens of public libraries throughout the Empire, but after Rome fell, one chronicler wrote: 'That libraries, like tombs, were shut up forever.' If it hadn't been for the Irish monasteries and the monks in them, the culture, learning and writing could have been eradicated in Western Europe. Central to that transmission of learning were manuscripts. Soon every monastery had its own scriptorium, where newly trained scribes copied and copied everything from the Old and New Testaments, to

Latin and Greek classics."[1]

Ireland thrived because of Celtic Christianity and the faith remained alive in parts of Britain, but most of Britannica was still lost in the darkness of the newly introduced paganism, brought by the Germanic tribes who seized most of England. For Patrick, his writings explain how he was consumed with fulfilling Jesus' Great Commission, to take the gospel to the ends of the earth, and Ireland was to him the very end of the world; and his converts wanted to follow his example.

Patrick reached further west than the Roman Empire and now his spiritual descendants took New Testament Christianity further north than the Romans, deep into Scotland, to the Kingdom of the unconquered Picts. As a first step, in AD 563 twelve chosen Celtic missionaries sailed from Ireland, to the Irish territories in Scotland in the Kingdom of Dál Riata, to set up a base for reaching the furthest extent of the known world.

Columba (521-597) was a descendant of the high kings of Ireland and as an aristocrat he could have lived the high life, but instead he chose to risk his life and serve Christ as a missionary. He was the head of the twelve missionaries to reach Scotland and when they landed, it was he who spoke to the King of Dál Riata and gained permission to be in his Kingdom. As an aristocrat, he could speak on equal terms with the king and gained liberty to travel, and he was also given some land, right on the edge of the Kingdom.

When I traversed the Island of Iona, I was struck by two things; first that a Christian witness has been present for over 1,400 years and second, there seemed to be many New Age tourists and possibly priests, who had forgotten the New Testament principles instilled by the missionaries that established this base.

In this harsh windswept region on the edge of the known world, Celtic Christianity thrived, combining a love of Scripture, education and living in the supernatural realm of God. Many myths have grown about the life of Columba, yet the stories which form the basis for the books on his prophetic revelations, his miraculous powers and his visions of angels, written down a century after his life, contain a seed truth of New Testament Christianity. Signs and wonders were certainly witnessed, but having been compiled long after his death, we cannot be sure exactly what took place. Yet without doubt these events provide us with shadows of the real servant of God, who experienced things similar to the apostles, as recorded in the book of Acts.

Like the apostle Paul, Peter and Jesus, Columba exercised the gifts of the Holy Spirit, and just as the first Church thrived and spread through the miraculous power of the Holy Spirit, so too did the Church in Britain (1 Corinthians 12:4-11). Peter received visions from God which led to conversions (Acts 10:1-16), Paul saw a vision of a Macedonian calling for help (Acts 16:9), and Jesus foresaw Nathanael before he met him (John 1:47-51). Columba and the Celtic believers were the same and they always returned to the Scriptures, not visions, for doctrine.

The Irish Gaels had been colonising parts of Scotland for some time and whilst under the protection of the Kingdom of Dál Riata or on Iona, these missionaries and their new followers had a sense of safety. This gave them time to sow a biblical foundation, to establish Christianity in all of Scotland. "It was nothing less than one of the most dynamic engines of Christianity in the world," said Dan Snow of the mission base of Iona, and the monks brought with them, "the seed of a new civilisation."[2]

After setting up the community on Iona which thrived and became a centre of civilisation, by the late 560s, Columba risked his life again by crossing into pagan Pictland. Piercing through the darkness and dangers of entering a savage Kingdom, which dominated the east and north of Scotland, Columba believed his message could transform the Kingdom.

The land of the Picts, like Ireland before Patrick, was still in the Iron Age, with stone carvings instead of literature, brutish pagan rituals and the warlike tribes were so fierce that the Roman Emperor Hadrian (AD 76-

138) ordered the construction of Hadrian's Wall to keep these barbarians out. The Picts refused to fight a conventional war with the Roman Empire, adopting guerrilla tactics that enabled them to inflict a defeat and disappear, and for this reason the Romans could never achieve supremacy. It was this land that Columba and his missionary band chose to enter, without protection, knowing that any angry warrior or tribe within, could capture, torture and kill them. It certainly was a dangerous mission into the pagan unknown ends of the earth.

As a miracle in and of itself, the team of missionaries crossed the land safely and stood before the gates of the pagan King Bridei, King of Fortriu, at his base in Inverness. The King of the Picts refused to hear their message, but through a series of miracles, the king changed his mind. Legend states Columba was barred from the city and by the miraculous intervention of God, the city gates opened, and the people within realised this new Divinity was the one and only true God. If something like this did happen, it mirrors the miracles which enabled Peter to keep on preaching (Acts 5:19).

"He established that the power of the King of kings (Jesus Christ) is greater than the King of the Picts," explains Dr James Fraser. "Columba and the Christian God has established their power...the greater of the two kings, the King of kings is brought to bare against the King of the Picts and there's only going to be one winner in that kind of confrontation. The King of the Picts is presented with this much more powerful force outside of his gates and he has no real opportunity to do anything, but to submit...There's an obvious power here that the Picts must recognise. This Divinity has got real power...this is a powerful religion, this is a powerful God."[3]

Nevertheless, the pagan druids or wizards, as some called them, realised they were the losers in this confrontation and refused to accept Columba's authority. As a Christian, Columba ordered the chief druid to free all slaves and he refused. Exactly what happened is lost in elaborate chronicles of a later age, but the result is self-evident – paganism was defeated and the Christian God was accepted as greater than all the other gods or spirits. From this encounter the message spread to the Picts that Christianity was a potent and muscular religion, with a great God, who cared about freeing the poorest person in the land and could break the power of the druids.

With Columba and his team now accepted into the heart of the Kingdom, modernity, prosperity and civilisation flourished. With Christianity thriving and uniting the peoples, the foundations were laid for the formation of the Kingdom of Scotland.

As a man of faith and education, Columba was able to help the King of the Picts build peaceful relationships with the wider world, and as a renowned man of letters, he is credited with writing several hymns and transcribing hundreds of books. "Celtic Christianity took off in a spectacular way all over the western British isles," explains Dr Robert Bedford, "creating a network of monasteries, which stretched from Iona in the north to the Bay of Biscay…against a background of traditionally Celtic culture, learning and literature flourished. What's more, these Celtic monasteries sent out missionaries."[4]

Germanic invaders had spiritually bankrupted England with their pagan darkness, but now the Celtic roots which survived the collapse re-emerged to reconnect England with its old faith. From these centres, Celtic missionaries marched throughout Scotland and into England to preach Jesus Christ. Meanwhile, Augustine landed in England seeking converts and won many.

Out of all the Anglo-Saxon territories, the Kingdom of Northumbria, in north east England and south east Scotland was to become powerful. King Edwin (586-633), ruled this Kingdom and converted to Christianity having been baptised in 627. His reign became far more peaceful, but he was killed in battle with pagans just six years later. The Kingdom was divided and King Oswald of Northumbria (604-642) desired to see it united.

Young Oswald was a man of deep faith. He spent years

as an exile living in the Christian communities in Ireland and Iona, and there he converted to Christianity. He fled as a twelve year old boy and when he reached thirty, he was ready to return and was determined that the Kingdom of Northumbria was to be Christian in nature. He sent for missionaries and the first was too harsh and the people could not accept him, so a second was sent.

The Celtic missionary Aidan (590-651) believed the first mission expected too much, too soon from the pagans, and instead followed the example of Isaiah, seeking little by little, precept upon precept (Isaiah 28:10). Aidan was hugely successful as a preacher and history calls him Aidan of Lindisfarne, because he established a church on the island of Lindisfarne in 635 and it became a centre of civilisation, trade and learning, based upon Christianity.

King Oswald of Northumbria embraced the Christian faith to the full and he translated Aidan's sermons to share them with the rich and powerful in his Kingdom. Also, King Oswald prayed for a united Kingdom and he believed only God could give him the victory against the aggressors who had divided Northumbria.

Whilst deep in prayer, King Oswald received a vision of Columba, who had died over three decades previously, giving him a word from God, saying something similar to the words given to Joshua by the Lord, "Be strong and act manfully. Behold, I will be with thee. This coming night go out from your camp into battle, for the Lord has granted me that at this time, your foes shall be put to flight and Cadwallon your enemy shall be delivered into your hands, and you shall return victorious after battle and reign happily" (Joshua 1:9).

King Oswald shared his vision with his council and all agreed that if God gave them the victory, as the supernatural revelation explained, they would all convert to Christianity. Before the battle commenced, King Oswald knelt before a wooden cross he planted in front of all, and then he prayed to the Lord, asking for His aid, and King Oswald asked all his army to join in. He cried out, "Let us all kneel and jointly beseech the true and living God Almighty, in His mercy, to defend us from the haughty and fierce enemy; for He knows that we have undertaken a just war for the safety of our nation."[5]

The subsequent great victory secured the future of Christianity in the north of England and southern Scotland, and from the new centres of faith, Celtic missionaries brought the gospel message to the British people. They taught confidence in the Scriptures, faith in Christ and they experienced the supernatural power of God in dreams, visions and revelations (Acts 2:17-18).

"Christianity had an enormous impact on all people in Anglo-Saxon society, at all levels," explains Professor Sarah Foot, "but I suppose one of the appeals about Christianity was it does offer an answer to that eternal question – why are we here, is this all there is, will there be anything afterwards? It offers a promise of eternal life and salvation beyond the life in this world, and perhaps an eternal life that is a little more egalitarian than the life they are living now in the world. And also of course, a heavenly existence that gets rid of social class distinctions in a way that pagan views of the after-world – which tend to perpetuate the idea that the warrior elite will have a particular enjoyable time in the afterlife – Christianity alters that view."[6]

"It's an absolutely fundamental change," says Professor Sarah Foot, "you could argue that there is really no aspect of life, at any social level in Anglo-Saxon England that isn't affected by the change to Christianity. People's worship patterns change! If they're going to follow the teaching of the Church, then they're going to start living their lives in different ways... it infiltrates every single aspect of daily life... The Church brings technologies unknown in England... everything about life in England is fundamentally changed. You could argue it was one of the most important things in the British Isles, in the first millennium – the conversion to Christianity."[7]

Wilfred of York (633-709), who originally trained at Lindisfarne also reintroduced written law in England. "He's one of those people who are transforming the legal culture of Anglo-Saxon England," said Dr Martin Ryan, "the use of written documents like charters to prove possession of land. We see it at the same time, law codes coming into existence; the first law code at the start of the seventh century with the conversion to Christianity. We find charters surviving from Anglo-Saxon England from the 670s and 680s. So he's transforming the culture and its becoming a culture based upon the written word. Law is written now, so you need legal documents."[8]

Celtic Christianity, grounded in Scripture flourished in Ireland, Scotland, England and Wales, and the home-grown missionary endeavours enabled the pure gospel, which had been first brought to England along the Roman roads, to be transmitted all over Britain, to the various kingdoms and territories.

A nation which became filled with pagan darkness soon began producing the most outstanding works of art and literature, based upon the Bible. Art historian Dr Janina Ramirez said that the *Lindisfarne Gospels* are, "The finest piece of art from the Dark Ages and a national treasure...this one manuscript is the culmination of centuries of Anglo-Saxon endeavour." It shows elements of native Celtic and Roman Christianity. "Today the *Lindisfarne Gospels* are considered one of the world's greatest art works."[9]

Chapter Five

The Celtic Mission to Europe

Whilst in parts of Europe, the darkness of the legacy of the Germanic pagan expansion was still stifling progress, soon, a series of missions from Ireland and Britain would change the course of European history. Celtic Christianity was to spread from Ireland and Britain into Europe!

"One of the great things about Ireland in this period, is the relationship that it enjoyed with the European mainland," said Dr John Moreland, "and many, many scholars coming from the European mainland to attend and study in Irish monasteries; but of course, the other process going on – of Irish monasteries going out on a great wave of monastic foundations in Europe, in the early medieval period." It led to "the re-introduction of Christianity into many parts of continental Europe"[1] after the pagan invasions.

Celtic Christian monks, spearheading the pinnacle of European education, were called for and sent into Europe. They opened up monasteries and their books flourished in Europe. In France, their monastery at Luxeuil became the Oxford of its time and Bobbio in Italy became Cambridge, with a huge library. In St Gallen, Switzerland, an architectural blueprint for an Irish Celtic monastery was found – it's the only one known to survive since the fall of Rome. This was the foundation of a new civilisation in Europe, based upon Celtic Christian faith, education and design.

In Britain, the Celtic Golden Age created the greatest light of this period.[2] Whilst the Dark Age was deep in much of Europe, in Britain and Ireland, Celtic Christianity produced a civilisation far ahead of its time. At its peak the monks on Iona produced the *Book of Kells*, a masterpiece containing the four Gospels, which was the combination of the zenith of known science, literature and art coalesced. In this age, the *Book of Kells* was just as important and pioneering as the Moon Landing, the works of Shakespeare and the Mona Lisa combined. With light bursting forth all over Britain, people from Europe wanted to learn and train under the leadership of Celtic Christians.

"The English Golden Age shone and became a beacon which shone, not just in these islands, but across Europe too," said Dr Robert Bedford. "English missionaries masterminded Christianity's expansion into what was then pagan Austria and Germany." Alcuin of York (735-804), from the Kingdom of Northumbria, at the invitation of the King of the Franks Charlemagne (742-814) of Germany, became the leading scholar and teacher at the Carolingian Court of this new and vast European empire. He began to lead them in Christianity and law, and Charlemagne spread the faith around his empire. "The Holy Roman Empire was the result," said Dr Robert Bedford, "a new Christian empire that would rule on the continent of Europe for a thousand years... English Christians had achieved so much and wielded so much influence over European affairs."[3]

However and this is a great however, Celtic Christianity did not survive to become the dominant Christian influence in Britain or Europe; in fact, it didn't survive at all. Two factors caused its downfall – the rise of a centralised religious authority in Rome, bringing all churches in Western Europe under its influence and the invasion of the Vikings into Britain from the north. To understand the former, we must evaluate the legacy of the first Christian emperor in Rome.

Chapter Six

A New Brand of Faith

In AD 306, far off on the edge of the known world, in the Province of Britannia, one young Roman ruler was set to change the world. He bravely fought the Picts far into unknown Scotland and it was in York, England, where Constantine the Great (272-337) was proclaimed Augustus. A statue of him resides by York Minster Cathedral stating: 'Near this place, Constantine the Great was proclaimed Roman Emperor in 306. His recognition of the civil liberties of his Christian subjects and his own conversion to the faith established the religious foundations of Western Christendom.' However, he was not the only man who claimed the right to rule the entire Roman Empire. Michael Portillo, broadcaster and former Cabinet Minister explains, "Because of the enormity of the Empire, it had four co-rulers. Constantine governed Britain, Gaul and Spain,"[1] and now he wanted absolute rule over all the Roman Empire.

In 312, Constantine crossed his own Rubicon towards death or victory, and was on the outskirts of Rome, seeking to take control of the whole Empire from his surviving rival Maxentius (278-312). The historian James Gerrard tells us what happened next: 'The story that has survived centuries describes how Constantine, worried by the size of his enemy's army, sought aid from the gods and was rewarded by the appearance in the sky of a flaming cross. Later that night God came to the pagan Constantine in a dream and told him, "By this sign conquer." The next day when Constantine went into battle with Maxentius, his troops bore crosses on their shields and carried a Christian standard before them. They were victorious and Constantine, after another murderous bout of civil war, emerged as the sole and first Christian ruler of the Roman World.'[2]

- 45 -

The conversion of Constantine to Christianity was either the greatest triumph of Christianity over the Roman Empire, or its bleakest disaster. Critics tell us that having failed to persecute the Christian faith to death, Rome was able to give it all that was needed to corrupt it – money, power and political influence. Those who look to the good, tell us that Constantine stopped the violent and bitter persecution of Christians, enabled the slow transition of Europe from paganism towards Christianity, built churches, and brought the bishops together in peace to safeguard orthodoxy and enable the duplication of the validated Scriptures. By AD 313, the Edict of Milan legalised Christianity across the whole Empire and safeguarded toleration for all.

"The conversion of Constantine was the single most important political event in the history of the Church," argues Michael Portillo. According to his admirers, Constantine enabled the Christianisation of Europe. He brought Christian leaders together to identify the valid letters and books of the apostles, and he had fifty copies made to safeguard them; thus securing them for posterity. Additionally, the doctrines found in Scripture were debated and confirmed, "But what was Constantine's true intention?" asks Portillo.[3]

When I stood by Milvian Bridge, in Italy, the site of the great battle which led to the conversion of Constantine, it seemed peculiar that this one battle in Rome would eventually lead to the sinking of Celtic Christianity in Britain, and the demise of all the independent Christian witnesses in Western Europe. On the Triumphal Arch of Constantine, next to the Coliseum, which was dedicated in AD 315 to his victory, I saw no Christian symbols or mention of Jesus. Instead, there is a vague reference to the 'divine.' The vague wording of Constantine's inscription may be understood as his attempt to please all possible readers, being deliberately ambiguous, and acceptable to both the majority pagans and the minority Christian population. Still visible in Latin is: 'To the Emperor Caesar Flavius Constantinus, the greatest, pious and blessed Augustus: because he, inspired by the divine, and by the greatness of his mind, has delivered the state from the tyrant and all of his followers at the same time, with his army and just force of arms, the Senate and People of Rome have dedicated this arch, decorated with triumphs.'

Author and religious commentator Jonathan Bartley said, "This is one of the most tragic periods for Christianity. It completely changes the meaning of Christianity. For example, Christians go from loving their enemies, as Jesus told them to, to killing them on the battlefield and then praying for them. They go from setting slaves free to endorsing a system of slavery. They go from being opposed to torture, to actually being part of those who do the imprisoning. This is a complete one hundred and eighty degree turn. Under Constantine Christianity goes from being something which opposes the Empire, to being part of the Empire and then indeed, you have to be a Christian in order to be part of the Empire at all."[4]

Michael Portillo concluded about this historic transmutation, "Rather than Constantine converting the Empire to Christianity, it might be more accurate to say he converted Christianity to his needs as an emperor."[5]

At this point, Christians in the Roman Empire began to split into two groups; those who felt happy to be in power with Rome and the few, who felt the faith was being corrupted. Dr Caroline Humfress said, "Some Christians looked back to the early days of Christianity and they looked back to the time of the martyrs, and they believed the Empire should be separate from Christianity, and not everyone was delighted being in the centre of power."[6]

Like some of the leaders of Celtic Christianity in Britain, some followers of Jesus in the Roman Empire began to withdraw into the wilderness, rejecting its corrupt charm and sought purity. They decided it was better to become living martyrs, rejecting all power and wealth, to get to know God in the deserts and hills, and maybe return to preach, just as John the Baptist had. The monastic movement thus began, in protest.

For three hundred years Christians from Israel to Rome

had worshipped in their homes, or underground, in simple sacrificial faith, but now the Emperor Constantine began building great churches in Rome. The largest monolithic church, called St John the Lateran, was built like a palace fit for Caesar, combining the opulence of Roman design with its aureate wealth. The historian Elizabeth Lev said, "Not only did he construct the enormous building, but he also gave beautiful marble columns, he gave forty golden and silver chandeliers for the nave, he gave silver plate, gold plate candle sticks. So he filled the church with beautiful objects."[7] It was all lavishly flamboyant, but what had happened to Jesus of Nazareth, a carpenter's son?

Beginning with the Church of St John the Lateran, the wealth of the Christian world, usually drawn from the poor, was soon being spent on church and cathedral building projects. A new age had dawned and it looked wonderful to the human eye, but did any of it sit comfortably with Scripture?

The apostles James warned that it is very easy for Christians to begin to deny the basic principles of their faith, to be 'in' with the rich and powerful. 'My brethren, do not hold the faith of our Lord Jesus Christ, the Lord of glory, with partiality. For if there should come into your assembly a man with gold rings, in fine apparel, and there should also come in a poor man in filthy clothes, and you pay attention to the one wearing the fine clothes and say to him, "You sit here in a good place," and say to the poor man, "You stand there," or, "Sit here at my footstool," have you not shown partiality among yourselves, and become judges with evil thoughts? Listen, my beloved brethren: Has God not chosen the poor of this world to be rich in faith and heirs of the Kingdom which He promised to those who love Him? But you have dishonoured the poor man. Do not the rich oppress you and drag you into the courts? Do they not blaspheme that noble name by which you are called?' (James 2:1-7).

In Celtic Britain and Ireland, Christians followed the path of self-denial and had spread this faith all across

Britain, and exported it back into pagan areas of Europe. But now in Rome, a new kind of faith emerged from the emperor. After Constantine the Great, most of the emperors were Christians of a sort; only Julian (330-363) mounted a concerted action to re-instate paganism as the dominant religion. He failed to de-establish Christianity and by 392 Emperor Theodosius I (347-395) decreed that Christianity was to be the only legal religion of the Roman Empire. He banned pagan practices saying, "It is our will that all the peoples who are ruled by the administration of our clemency shall practice that religion which the divine Peter the Apostle transmitted to the Romans."[8]

But what about Celtic Christianity and all other free believers in Jesus Christ? Theodosius I introduces two ideas, first, Peter was the founder of the Church in Rome and second, all Christians have to follow Rome's centralised interpretation of Christianity, or be deemed 'insane' and 'heretical.' "The rest," Theodosius declared, "whom we adjudge demented and insane, shall sustain the infamy of heretical dogmas, their meeting places shall not receive the name of churches, and they shall be smitten first by divine vengeance and secondly by the retribution of our own initiative."[9]

Theodosius I helped invent the idea of Peter as the first Pope, as he ignored the fact that the Bible chronicles Paul was the first apostle in Rome. Paul ministered in the city for at least two years, laying the foundations for the Church (Acts 28:17-31). Theodosius also overlooked that Paul is the author of the Epistle to the Roman Christians. Meanwhile, Peter's letters were addressed to believers in modern day Turkey and Greece (1 Peter 1:1). Why did Theodosius invent the concept of a Pope? Centralised Christianity adopted by an absolute emperor, also needed an absolute Christian leader. If Roman emperors were going to harness Christianity for their own ends, they needed a centralised system which they could control.

When Rome was sacked in AD 410 by barbarians, a political and spiritual void was created by the weakened

Roman leadership. Michael Portillo said, "Whilst in the East Church and state remained as one, in the West, Rome fell to the Barbarians and into that imperial vacuum stepped a new power that is still with us today, the Papacy."[10] From Theodosius' aided invention of a centralised faith, to the day Rome fell and the Bishop of Rome stepped into that void, the apostolic style of the New Testament was diminished in favour of following the Roman emperor's top down style of leadership.

Just as the Roman Republic gave way to an absolute emperor, so too, apostolic New Testament Christianity gave way to an absolute spiritual leader. "It enabled the Christian Church to develop a hierarchy very rapidly," explains Dr Caroline Humfress, "the Pope in Rome assumes a certain position, which is almost comparable to the one which the emperor has in the Roman world."[11]

The apostles were renegades in the Roman Empire, yet now future Popes ruled what was left of it. "In the Western Empire Constantine's legacy is the Roman Catholic Church," concluded Michael Portillo. "Having enjoyed the protection of Constantine, the Church was now strong enough to prosper in Rome, long after its protectors passed into history. In 476, the puppet Emperor Romulus Augustus was disposed. There were to be no more Roman emperors in the West, until Charlemagne in the year 800. It was the Christian Church that benefited. Into the void, left by the collapse of the Empire in the West, stepped the Pope... by the seventh century, the Papacy is the largest land owner on the Italian peninsula and its armies were fully prepared to defend, and advance those territories."[12]

The Roman Emperor was now lost to history and the office of Pope was created in its likeness. In the chaos that followed, the bishops of Rome forgot what the Bible declared – that Peter was given the charge to give the gospel to the Jews and Paul to the Gentiles, and one leader took charge of all the Church. 'When they saw that the gospel for the uncircumcised had been committed to me, as the gospel for the circumcised was to Peter (for He who worked effectively in Peter for the apostleship to the circumcised also worked effectively in me toward the Gentiles)' (Galatians 2:7-8).

The word Pope is a derivative of the Greek word father. In the first three centuries, this title was common for all bishops; by the sixth century it was commonly applied to the Bishop of Rome, and by the late eleventh century Pope Gregory VII (1015-1085) issued a declaration which claimed the title for Rome alone. The earliest record in English of the title Pope dates to the mid-tenth century.

The metamorphism of Christianity was undertaken by Emperor Constantine and Rome became the centre of Christianity, and Jerusalem, where the first council of the apostles was held was ignored (Acts 15). Pope's now ruled the Church, but investing power into one symbol of all spiritual authority, eventually led to the abuses of indulgences, the introduction of doctrines contradictory to the teaching of the apostles, the crusades, inquisitions and many Popes used the power of ex-communication to control governments all over Europe. If Rome was to rule, what was going to happen to Celtic Christianity?

Chapter Seven

Supremacy

In the modern world, Catholic and Protestant are words loaded with history, but in the days of the apostles both were not known. At first, the disciples of Jesus were called followers of 'The Way' (Acts 9:2), and at Antioch, they found a new name: 'The disciples were first called Christians in Antioch' (Acts 11:26). By the second century a Greek word, Katholikos, originally meaning universal, was adopted as a way of describing the entire Church, and by the time of Constantine the Great, this word evolved into Catholic, or 'the universal' Church of Christ. For the bishops of Rome by the time of Constantine, claiming the word Catholic meant claiming authority over all Christians, regardless of how they became followers of Jesus. Thus to be Catholic no longer meant to be part of the universal Church of Christ, but to be under the authority of Rome.

Meanwhile in Britain, a series of independent Celtic Christians centres were flourishing. By retreating into Cornwall, Wales, western England, Scotland and Ireland, the Celtic Christians survived the pagan Germanic invasions and re-evangelised Britain. Centres like Iona and Lindisfarne became instrumental for training local missionaries to reach the people of Britain, and yet each centre remained largely independent. For hundreds of years this form of Christianity thrived in Britain and Ireland, but the centralisation of Christianity towards Rome was to have a far reaching effect for Celtic Christianity.

"The Empire had gone," said the historian Dan Snow, "but the adopted religion of Christianity had survived with the Pope as its head in Rome. Where the Irish monasteries were self-governing, the Papacy was all for centralised control. It had inherited not only Rome's bureaucracy, but also its imperial ambitions. It was steadily expanding its authority in Europe, but its influence stopped short of Britain and Ireland. A new Pope, the ambitious Gregory the Great (540-604) was determined to change all that and to make it happen, he dispatched a Papal mission to Britain."[1]

At the time of this mission, Britain was a patchwork network of kingdoms, some pagans in the far south, others Christian in north east England, Wales, Scotland and Ireland. Columba had led the mission that brought Celtic Christianity back and restored it into Britain, but just as he died in 597, Augustine of Canterbury (545-605) arrived in southern England with a Roman centralised version of Christianity, with the Pope as its head.

Augustine of Canterbury, not to be confused with Augustine of Hippo (354-430), managed to secure a meeting with Ethelbert King of Kent (560-616). The king's wife was already a Christian, so Augustine's teaching was not new and he converted. The mission headed north into the Kingdom of Essex and St Paul's Church was built in London, but the mission struggled to convince people and St Paul's was later burnt down in a pagan backlash. After initial success, the mission came to a standstill, and almost all the advances made were quickly reversed. The greatest success was King Ethelbert's conversion and his new Christian law code, but his son and successor wavered between paganism and Christianity.

Augustine's greatest achievement was the mass baptism of ten thousand Anglo-Saxons, but their conversion shows all the signs of a political synthesis, rather than a hand-on-heart conversion. In the British Museum, the silver and gold buckle, originally from Crundale Down, Kent, tells another story.[2] Art historian Dr Janina Ramirez said, "In the British Museum is one of the best examples that shows how readily the Anglo-Saxons were prepared to follow both Christ and Wôdan... The silver and guilt belt buckle from Crundale Kent, is a serious piece of double-edged art," fusing pagan and Christian symbols. "This piece clearly shows it was made at a time when the Anglo-Saxons were hedging their bets; embracing Christianity and keeping hold of their pagan heritage...you can imagine the man who commissioned it – one week he is fasting for Easter, the next he is feasting for the goddess Ēostre."[3]

Augustine's mission came close to utter failure when he met with Celtic Christian leaders in Britain. Augustine knew of these native believers because Pope Gregory had proudly 'given him' authority over all the Celtic Christians, but he was surprised by their size and strength. He expected them all to quickly recognise the authority of the Pope, "but the Celtic Christians in the West rejected Augustine's Roman authority," explains Dr Robert Bedford.[4]

For Augustine this was tantamount to heresy and the exchange became bitter. "He really tried to bully them," explains Professor Nicholas Higham, "persuasion is not a strong enough word I think." In a reversal of his intention, the harsher and harder Augustine's claims were made, the more the Celtic Christians believed this man and all he stood for was not Christ-like, but imperial. "In this particular case they eventually say, 'No! You are not sufficiently a humble man for us to accept as our leader,' " explains Professor Nicholas Higham. "They rejected him. The mission came extremely close to total failure."[5]

Celtic Christianity had more than half a millennia of living heritage in Britain, as it drew from almost six centuries of history. What they had received hundreds of years before was an independent witness of Christ, free from any tainted influence of the Roman Emperor Constantine, or any legacy from the Roman Empire. The heritage they embraced seemed quite different from the new concepts of a Pope, with centralised authority and a claim that Rome was still the centre of the world. "The problem with Augustine's Roman Christianity was that it was an alien force imposed on the people of Britain," said Dr Robert Bedford. "It was rejected by the people he came to convert and even by the Celtic Christians."[6]

Nevertheless, King Ethelbert's conversion was Augustine's great legacy, because at least one southern Kingdom in England would survive the Viking terror of the future, and the convictions sown into these hearts would live on. But in the present hour, a spiritual battle commenced for supremacy in Britain. Would the independent Celtic communities remain or would Roman Christianity, the legacy of the Roman Empire take charge?

In the north of England and southern Scotland, King Oswald of Northumbria (604-642) established his large Kingdom as Christian and encouraged the Celtic missionary Aidan to send out his missionaries to re-evangelise Britain. However, thirteen years after Aidan's death and twenty-two years after King Oswald's death, leaders from Rome met with Celtic Christian leaders at the Synod of Whitby, in Yorkshire, on the east coast of England to decide the future of Christianity in Britain.

The Synod of Whitby was not an obscure theological debate, which had no other meaning; it was as substantial European conference. It was the G7 of its day, and the questions being asked were as important as, "Should Britain join the European Union and the Euro?" If the answer was "Yes," British Christians would become part of a worldwide universal or Catholic Church, and like the European Union of today, there would be many benefits, and drawbacks. If accepted, British bishops could travel to Rome and sit as equals with Roman Catholic bishops, but to do this, they would have to give up their authority and the legacy of Celtic Christianity. Just like the European Union, any nation which wants to join has to give up their absolute claim on sovereignty to be in the club.

The Synod was held in the Kingdom of Northumbria, the most powerful Kingdom in Britain. King Oswiu (612-670) was now residing and he listened to the arguments put before him. Wilfrid (633-709) was born in Northumbria and studied at Lindisfarne, but he later studied in Rome, and he argued the case that Britain had to submit to the authority of Rome. Colmán of

Lindisfarne (605-675) believed God had birthed Celtic Christianity and it must remain independent to Him.

Christianity was established in Britain by missionary minded prophets and apostles like Patrick and Columba, with signs following to confirm the Word, and now a politician was going to decide the future of the British Church!

The historian Bede tells us what happened. Wilfrid argued the Celtic Church was, "In obstinacy, I mean the Picts and the Britons, who foolishly, in these two remote islands of the world, and only in part even of them, oppose all the rest of the universe."[7] Colmán thought it was odd that a fellow believer would mock what God achieved in Britain, saying, "It is strange that you will call our labours foolish."[8] Wilfrid argued that the date of Easter, kept by the Celtic Church was out of sync with the testimony of Scripture.

For Colmán, he believed the signs and wonders given by God were the proof that God blessed them. "Is it to be believed that our most reverend Father Columba and his successors, men beloved by God, who kept Easter after the same manner, thought or acted contrary to the Divine writings?" he asked. "Whereas there were many among them, whose sanctity is testified by heavenly signs and the working of miracles, whose life, customs, and discipline I never cease to follow, not questioning their being saints in heaven."[9]

Colmán points to the central problem of Roman Christianity – it was for the Celtic believers, too worldly, lusting for power and undisciplined. It was the son of the Roman Empire; Christianity in Britain was the child of God, birthed by men and women led by the Holy Spirit to preach. But Wilfred for Rome warned all the Christians that they could find themselves outside the fold of Christ. "But as for you and your companions, you certainly sin, if, having heard the decrees of the Apostolic See, and of the universal Church, and that the same is confirmed by holy writ, you refuse to follow them. For, though your fathers were holy, do you think that their small number, in a corner of the remotest island, is to be preferred before the universal Church of Christ throughout the world?"[10]

"This is one of the most violent synods recorded in the Anglo-Saxon Church and it certainly sounds as if tempers did get quite hot," said Professor Sarah Foot. "There's a phenomenal amount at stake here. Making a decision about when you should celebrate the central festival of the Christian religion, there's nothing bigger...it's making a decision if you want to side with Iona and the Church in Ireland, or whether you want to join the European cultural mainstream."[11]

'Conflict between the Roman and Celtic Churches in Britain was inevitable,' explains the historian and expert on Anglo-Saxon England, Peter Hunter Blair. 'During its long period of isolation the Celtic Church had developed in complete independence and had diverged considerably from the paths followed by Rome, not merely in the matters of form and ritual, but more fundamentally in its whole organisation. Rome could not readily brook the continued existence of what it regarded as schismatic ways and still less could it contemplate so large a Christian community which showed remarkable missionary zeal should not recognise the Pope as its spiritual head. But on the other side, the Celtic Church, as some of its members realized, could not afford to ignore the benefits which Rome, representing by far the greater part of Christendom, had to offer.'[12]

For half a millennia Celtic Christians were free, some having been led by their spiritual leaders of austere, sacrificial faith. These servants of God proved the power of God was working through them in miracles. The prophets of the Bible and the apostles taught that spiritual leadership could not be inherited, like a title, but had to be proved by God's power working through you. Paul's case that he was not an "inferior" apostle, as some had taught (because he had not met Jesus in the flesh), because the signs and wonders God had sent through him were his evidence. 'Truly the signs of an apostle were accomplished among you with all perseverance, in signs and wonders and mighty deeds'

(2 Corinthians 12:12-13). Paul argued that clever people can win debates, yet God confirms His Word by sending signs and miracles. 'My speech and my preaching were not with persuasive words of human wisdom, but in demonstration of the Spirit and of power, that your faith should not be in the wisdom of men but in the power of God' (1 Corinthians 2:4-5).

However, the future of Christianity in Britain was in the hands of a king and he had more than theology to concern himself with. King Oswiu ruled in favour of Rome, when he became convinced of the doctrine that Peter was the first Pope and the Rock of the Church (Matthew 16:18-19). "He's clearly trying to ingratiate himself with the Pope in Rome," said Professor Sarah Foot, "there's a correspondence with the Pope and his decision means he is siding permanently on behalf of the Roman Church...it makes the date of Easter the same all the way across Western Europe. It's like making a decision to join a central European currency; it's a currency of faith."[13]

A king decided the fate of Christianity in Britain and the leaders of the Celtic Church retreated into obscurity. Celtic Christianity, originally founded on New Testament principles, was dying and it would soon be dead. Perhaps they had strayed from the founding principles of the faith, or it was a time of falling away in the Church. Nevertheless, the Celtic legacy in art, literature and faith would hang on for at least two centuries, but it suffered a two-fold death – foreign spiritual supremacy from the south and pagan invasions from the north.

With Celtic Christianity giving way to Roman Christianity, a new form of Church building spread across Britain. Dr Janina Ramirez said, "A century after St Augustine landed, stone symbols of the Christian faith began to dominate the landscape. In the wooden world of the Anglo-Saxons, stone crosses made a big impact. This proved to be an effective advertising campaign, one that definitely said paganism was fading away and Christianity was here to stay. New churches and Abbey's sprung up throughout the Anglo-Saxon lands."[14]

St Martin's Church in Canterbury is the oldest stone church in Britain and is still in use, with a history of worship stretching back at least fourteen hundred years. The building resides where an ancient church once stood and it was renovated in stone by 580. As the building pre-dated Augustine's mission, he chose it as his base camp. Nearly sixty years later, Augustine's work resulted in the second stone church in Britain, called the Chapel of St Peter-on-the-Wall, in Bradwell-on-Sea, Essex, which was mentioned by Bede.[15] This was the beginning of the new architectural appearance of Britain, with stone church buildings dotted all over the land.

After the initial wave of missionaries from Rome, others followed and the grip of Roman faith on the nation began to take hold. The Celtic believers had lost out to an internationally recognised faith, and as each year passed, people gave up a little of their history, to embrace the new European way of doing things. As Roman traditions were introduced the apostolic legacy was lost further in rituals, relics, ceremonies and hierarchies.

Wilfred was the great winner in this battle between Celtic faith and Roman faith, and to the winner went the spoils! "Along with their rules, relics and architecture came the Roman Church's pomp and hierarchy," said Dr Janina Ramirez. "Wilfrid's lavish ostentation was in stark contrast to the Spartan lives of the Celtic monks of Skellig. Wilfrid was a foretaste of what monasteries and the monks who ran them would become. Hexham Abbey was his palace. He would have dressed like a king, wearing the brightest vestments made of the finest fabrics and silk brought in from the Continent. He even had his throne made, modelled on the sorts of thrones he'd seen from abbots and bishops in France. I don't think it's a coincidence that he had it made of reclaimed Roman stone. The Roman Empire has now become the Christian Roman Empire. Romulus and Remus have been replaced by Peter and Paul, and a bishop is now a spiritual king."[16]

Celtic Christianity had long suffered from the exchange

with the Roman brand of faith, and its biblical heritage was watered-down as each generation tried to adopt the ways of their sophisticated European neighbours. But now the whole of Christianity in Britain was obliged to be inside Europe and to submit to the European way of doing things, and the heritage of the faith of the disciples from Israel and the Middle East began to fade. Nevertheless the centralised order of the Roman brand of the faith enabled new scholarship to thrive.

The Venerable Bede was convinced of the good the Roman faith could bring and in his book *The Ecclesiastical History of the English*, which was completed in 731, the Celtic Christians were regarded with suspicion. Bede served in the Christian Kingdom of Northumbria as a monk and due to his historical writings he gained the title of The Father of English History.

In his book Bede presented a prophetic vision that the various kingdoms of England were destined by God to be one united nation, defined by Christianity. The historian Professor Diarmaid MacCulloch said, "It was a monk who first applied this concept of a nation chosen by God to the English, before the English as a people even existed." In Jarrow, Sunderland, "in what was the Anglo-Saxon Kingdom of Northumbria, the idea of England as God's chosen nation really began with the work of a monk who was the greatest historian of his age," he said. "His name was Bede and in the course of his life as a monk he wrote books that more than anything else shaped the soul of the English...what Bede wrote here did nothing less than invent the English...what's intriguing about this history, is that Bede was describing something that doesn't actually exist...the Anglo-Saxon world wasn't a single nation, England, but a collection of kingdoms ruled by warlords, repeatedly at each others throats. Until Bede wrote this history there was no such thing as the English. Even less a people united by God."[17]

When Bede read the Bible's description of Solomon's Temple he "saw meaning for his own land," explains Professor Diarmaid MacCulloch, "it had been built after once warring tribes were united into one holy nation, chosen by God, Israel, and from that unity followed wealth and God's protection. Now all that resonated with Bede and now he applied it to his own people. So Bede gave the Angles, the English, the idea that they would be a chosen people. It was a vision rich with possibilities. But a vision was all it was. It just needed someone to take it out of the dusty library and make it real and one of England's greatest mediaeval leaders did just that: Alfred the Great."[18]

Celtic Christianity had seeded Christianity back into Britain and Europe, "but then, at the very height of their success, disaster struck," said Dr Robert Bedford.[19] Roman Christianity was now the accepted brand and from the north fierce Viking warriors began landing in Britain, attacking all. The monasteries, as centres of civilisation were targeted and Iona was sacked several times. The Vikings showed no mercy to the Lord's servants and on one raid they took sixty-eight monks to the beach at Iona and brutally murdered them. Within fifty years of the first Viking attack on Iona in 794, its light was snuffed out. "Even Lindisfarne was sacked," explains Dr Robert Bedford, "by the 870s, only the Kingdom of Wessex survived. It was ruled by a man who would become a national hero. His name was Alfred. There seems for Alfred, there was no doubt this was not your usual Dark Age squabble. It was an apocalyptic battle between the forces of good and the forces of evil. A battle for the very survival of Christian England."[20]

Chapter Eight

King Alfred and Christianity

Throughout the centuries many kings in the divided kingdoms in Britain converted to Christianity, beginning with King Ethelbert in 597. There were several pagan lapses and by the 870s, the entire legacy of Christianity in the nation was about to be completely eradicated. Only one king was standing and he was hiding in the marshes of southern England. The pagan Viking attacks beginning in the north of Britain were catastrophic for Celtic and Roman Christianity, and for all the Anglo-Saxons and Celts. One by one, all the great kingdoms of the nation fell.

Alfred, King of Wessex was the last king standing in England and he was in retreat, running for his life. Whilst he hid in the marshes in Somerset, he gave himself to prayer and pondered why the Christian kingdoms of Britain had fallen to the pagans. His conclusion was that God Almighty had no use for a backslidden, half-hearted compromise between Christianity, worldliness and the remnants of paganism. In his view, Christians and their kings had not served the God of the Bible and for this reason His protection was removed from them. What God needs a people who claim to serve Him, but in practice rebel? How can a Christian Kingdom truly represent its God, whilst they remain ignorant or scornful of His will? "Alfred was convinced there could be no victory without God," explains Professor Diarmaid MacCulloch.[1]

One ancient thousand year old account tells us what happened when Alfred prayed about the collapse of the Christian kingdoms of Britain. Whilst he was on the run King Alfred showed kindness to a strange visitor who was in need, and he later believed that this needy 'man' was sent from heaven because Alfred was shaken by what he said (Hebrews 13:2).

The chronicler relays this account: 'Alfred alone lay awake in his bed, thinking with a sad heart of his sufferings and exile, and wondering much about the stranger and the unexpected draught of fishes. With a sudden a light from heaven, brighter than the beams of the sun, shone upon his bed. Struck with terror, he forgot all his former anxieties and looked in amazement on the brightness of the light. In the midst of which there appeared an elderly man, bearing the clerical fillet on his black locks, but having a most benignant look, and bearing in his right hand a copy of the Holy Gospels, adorned most marvellously with gold and jewels. He advanced and calmed the fears of the astonished king with these words, "Let not the brilliancy of my coming disturb you, beloved King Alfred, nor the fear of barbarian cruelty any longer harass you. For God, who does not despise the groans of His poor servants, will soon put an end to your troubles, and I, from henceforth, will be your constant helper."

'The king was comforted by these words and asked him earnestly who he was, and why he had come. Then the elderly man, smiling, said, "I am he to whom you this day ordered bread to be given; but I took not so much pleasure in the bread and wine, as in the devotion of your soul. But, whereas you ask me my name, know that I am Cuthbert, the servant of God, and am sent to explain to you, in familiar terms, how you may be relieved from the persecution, which has so long afflicted you." '[2]

When Alfred was in trouble and all the kingdoms of Britain were almost lost, he received a vision of the former Bishop of Lindisfarne, who served during the Celtic Golden Age in Britain. Cuthbert (634-687) was born in southern Scotland and served in the Church in the Northumbrian Kingdom, in the austere Celtic tradition. Cuthbert moved in signs and wonders, and like many in the Celtic Church balanced a belief in Divine inspiration from God in dreams and visions for his personal revelation, with a solid commitment to Scripture for orthodoxy.

King Alfred shared the same outlook – a commitment to the Scriptures for all doctrine and a belief in personal revelation from God. In the vision Alfred received, Cuthbert told him that God would eventually unify the whole of Britain because of his legacy. He said, "I advise you to cherish mercy and justice, and to teach them to your sons above everything else, seeing that at your prayer God has granted to you the disposal of the whole of Britain... Now put off your fears and inactivity, and as soon as tomorrow's light shall dawn, cross over to the nearest shore, and blow loudly with your horn three times. And as wax melts before the heat of the fire, so by your blasts shall the pride of your enemies, with God's will, be dissolved, and the courage of your friends be aroused."[3]

King Alfred followed the leading he received and like the Old Testament heroes, prepared his men to fight (Joshua 6:4). He spoke these words to the soldiers before the great battle to save England from complete Viking domination, "Let us be faithful to God, eschew evil, love the practice of virtue and so shall we everywhere experience the benefit of His protection."[4]

After a period of preparation, King Alfred, with deep repentance in prayer, led his new army out to battle, in the name of saving Christianity in the nation, to honour God. It was May 878 and in the Battle of Edington, an army of the Anglo-Saxon Kingdom of Wessex, under its newly committed Christian king, defeated the heathen army led by Guthrum. Alfred, in the name of God, not only saved Wessex, he saved England and Christianity in Britain.

The Vikings came as close as anyone ever had, to destroying Christianity in Britain. But God answered King Alfred's prayers and from now on, England was to be a true Christian nation, with the Bible at the heart of its law, culture, religion and identity.

After his victory over the Vikings, King Alfred could have continued in the pagan traditions and killed his enemies, but as a Christian, he followed the teaching of

Christ, to love his enemies and do good to those that hurt you (Matthew 5:44).

King Alfred invited Guthrum, his defeated pagan foe and many of his dishevelled enemies to a twelve day celebration, where they were honoured. When it was all over, Guthrum and his men left the celebration as baptised Christians! Guthrum's pagan tribe renounced their god Wôdan and worshipped Jesus Christ from then on, laying the bedrock for a united Christian England to emerge.

Under the terms of the Treaty of Wedmore in 878, the Viking Guthrum returned to his Kingdom in East Anglia, as a believer in Jesus Christ, and his new faith in God helped the two Kingdoms live in peace. England now had one common belief which united the two great Kingdoms – Christianity, and this strong faith laid the foundations for the future unification of the two Kingdoms into one, called England.

Winston Churchill (1874-1965) explains the significance of King Alfred's victory: 'The Christians, before they endured any such distress, by the inspiration of heaven judged it to be better either to suffer death or to gain the victory...if the West Saxons had been beaten, all England would have sunk into heathen anarchy. Since they were victorious the hope still burned for a civilised Christian existence in this Island.'[5]

To be a civilised people Alfred introduced the rule of law and sought to develop his Kingdom along biblical lines, and this had a significant impact on the pagan converts: 'The Christian culture of his Court sharply contrasted with the feckless barbarism of Viking life,' explains Winston Churchill. 'The older race was to tame the warriors and teach them the arts of peace, and show them the value of a settled common existence. We are watching the birth of a nation. The result of Alfred's work was the future mingling of Saxon and Dane in a common Christian England.'[6]

King Alfred built forts all around his Kingdom in England and began the process of developing the foundations of a coherent, peaceful land, based on the rule of law, sourced from the Bible. Professor Diarmaid MacCulloch explains Alfred believed God "would look with much favour on the nation if it knew His laws and obeyed them. Alfred's solution was to draw up a law code based on the Old Testament." His conviction was, "Keep God's laws and God will defend you against His enemies. In this cold northern island a new biblical identity was beginning to set firm."[7]

One fifth of King Alfred's law code, entitled the *Doom Book* – the Anglo-Saxon for law or judgment, contains King Alfred's introduction concerning his reasons for establishing a Kingdom based on Christianity. He directly copied Scripture, transcribing it into his law. He includes as foundational, the English translation of the Ten Commandments, plus several chapters from the book of Exodus. Alfred enabled England to embrace in law, the principle of justice for all and codified rules for justice which are still unavailable for most in the world today.

"You shall not circulate a false report. Do not put your hand with the wicked to be an unrighteous witness. You shall not follow a crowd to do evil; nor shall you testify in a dispute so as to turn aside after many to pervert justice. You shall not show partiality to a poor man in his dispute...and you shall take no bribe, for a bribe blinds the discerning and perverts the words of the righteous" (Exodus 23:1-3, 8).

England's law was defined by the Bible and impartial justice was at its heart. King Alfred also noted that his Kingdom was not to be Jewish in nature, but Christian, as he cites the letter written by the apostles to the Gentile believers in Jesus Christ from Acts 15:23-29. This explains that Christians are not expected to follow Jewish tradition. King Alfred divided his legal code into precisely 120 chapters, a number with symbolic religious medieval biblical significance – being the age of Moses' death.

King Alfred embraced the principle of the Lord Jesus, "Do unto others as you would that they should do unto you" (Luke 6:31), and tried to simplify the concept for his uneducated people and make it law. This is how Alfred taught it to his people, "What ye will that other men should not do to you, that do ye not to other men." Alfred told them, "By bearing this precept in mind a judge can do justice to all men; he needs no other law books. Let him think of himself as the plaintiff and consider what judgment would satisfy him."

On my visit to Winchester, I found an idealised city with an ancient heart. Near the river stands the substantial statue of King Alfred the Great, with his sword held high in the air, to remember his victory and the sword of justice which he brought to England. In Winchester Cathedral, it is still possible to find the oldest parts of this place of worship in the crypt, dating back over a thousand years, and in the Old Minster, King Alfred the Great was buried. Jane Austin and Mary Tudor were also buried in the Cathedral.

"Winchester was his capital city," said Dr Janina Ramirez, "under Alfred, Winchester became the very model of Anglo-Saxon civilisation; a place where art and culture would flourish. During his reign King Alfred introduced many new concepts we take for granted today," laying the solid foundations for a vibrant and civilised state, founded on biblical Christianity. "During his twenty-eight years on the throne, Alfred made the building of new churches and monasteries a priority," explains Dr Janina Ramirez. "The Church and his faith was very important to Alfred, he believed the reason the Vikings had come to rape and pillage his land was simple; his people were not pious enough."[8]

King Alfred dreamed of the Celtic Golden Age in Britain and held a romantic view of how great the kingdoms of the nation had been. Britain, due to its biblical faith was once at the forefront of technology, science, learning, literature and art when Christianity flourished in the Celtic Age, and people had come from all over Europe to learn in Ireland and Britain. Now Alfred wanted the dark cloud of paganism over England to lift in the name of Jesus Christ, to set the nation on the path towards being once again, a Christian civilisation.

King Alfred wrote the following: 'Let it be known to thee

that it has very often come into my mind, what wise men there formerly were throughout England, both of sacred and secular orders. And what happy times there were then throughout England; and how the kings who had power of the nation in those days obeyed God and His ministers. They preserved peace, morality and order at home, and at the same time enlarged their territory abroad. How they prospered both with war and with wisdom. And also the sacred orders, how zealous they were both in teaching and learning, and in all the services they owed to God. And how foreigners came to this land in search of wisdom and instruction, and how we should now have to get from abroad if we would have them.'[9]

Alfred was saddened that England was forced to look towards Europe for education and instruction, but he was grateful for the help received. 'So general was its decay in England that there were very few on this side of the Humber who could understand their rituals in English, or translate a letter from Latin into English,' lamented Alfred, 'there were so few that I cannot remember a single one south of the Thames when I came to the throne. Thanks be to God Almighty that we have teachers among us now. And therefore I command thee to do as I believe thou art willing, to disengage thyself from worldly matters as often as thou canst, that thou mayst apply the wisdom which God has given thee wherever thou canst. Consider what punishments would come upon us on account of this world, if we neither loved it ourselves nor suffered other men to obtain it. We should love the name only of Christian.'[10]

We remember King Alfred as the monarch who saved England and laid the foundations for a civilised Christian Britain, but during his reign, he lived through a true dark age, as the nation recovered from the pagan invasions. He dreamt of that lost Celtic Golden Age, writing: 'When I considered all this I remembered also how I saw, before it had been all ravaged and burnt, how the churches throughout the whole of England stood filled with books, and there was also a great multitude of

God's servants.' But sin led to the downfall of England. Alfred wrote: 'They had said, "Our forefathers, who formerly held these places, loved wisdom, and through it they obtained wealth and bequeathed it to us. In this we can still see their tracks, but we cannot follow them, and therefore have we lost all the wealth and the wisdom, because we would not incline our hearts after their example." '[11]

King Alfred was convinced the laws of God from the Bible had to be translated into English, so all could hear and understand the will of God. He concluded: 'Then I remember how the law was first known in Hebrew and again, when the Greeks had learnt it, they translated the whole of it into their own language, and all other books besides. And again, the Romans, when they had learnt it, they translated the whole of it through learned translators into their own language. And also all other Christian nations translated a part of them into their own language. Therefore it seems better to me, if ye think so, for us also to translate some books which are most needful for all men to know, into the language which we can all understand.'[12]

King Alfred is the only monarch in British history with the epitaph, 'The Great,' because his victory over the pagan armies saved the nation, and made sure that England was to be a truly Christian nation. "The battle achieved something else too," said Dr Robert Bedford, "it started the political unification of England. The Christian unity of the English people...was now a political reality. What was a religious and cultural community now became one nation, with one religion at its heart...These are the ideas that created not just England, but the nation [of Britain] which we know today. Our links to Alfred's Kingdom are deep. We owe to it – not just the monarchy and the Church, but the jury system, common law, even the counties we live in today. As a political entity, Hampshire is older than France...Those Dark Ages gave us a sense of national identity – one state, one language and up until recently, one religion. You don't find that in many countries, but you do in Britain because of what happened all those years ago. When out of the chaos and violence which followed the collapse of the Roman Empire, the peoples of Britain created a new idea of themselves, a Christian identity, which has made us what we are today. That's why I believe the Dark Ages are the most important in our history."[13]

King Alfred embraced a grand vision for the future of all the British kingdoms, working together as one, fused by Christianity. Professor Diarmaid MacCulloch said, "Alfred defeated the Vikings and he began to see himself, not as the king of one petty region, amidst a confusion of peoples, but as leading a whole chosen nation, bound by God's laws and only a quarter century after Alfred's death, it fell to his grandson, Athelstan, finally to make Bede proud. He transformed Bede's vision of a united English people from fantasy into reality. Athelstan was crowned with a new title – King of England. So it was an idea which created England, a biblical idea."[14]

Appendix A

Bishop Diaothus' Letter
The Independence of Celtic Christians

Saint Augustine was 'given' authority by the Pope over all Christians in Britain, but in his sixth century letter to Augustine, the Celtic Bishop Diaothus declares that the Celtic Church has never recognised any Roman religious authority over Britain. He notes the 'individual' Celtic Christian and the 'collective' faith of the Britons, and states they are only compelled to love all as equals. The Celtic Church has never been subject to any of these new entities, which includes these new terms such as 'Pope' or 'Bishop of Bishops.' The Celtic Church has its own leaders and it is free, as individuals and collectively.

Be it known and declared that we all, individually and collectively, are in all humility prepared to defer to the Church of God, and to the Bishop in Rome, and to every sincere Christian, so far as to love everyone according to his degree, in perfect charity, and to assist them all by word and in deed in becoming the children of God.

But as for any other obedience, we know of none that he, whom you term the Pope, or Bishop of Bishops, can demand. The deference we have mentioned we are ready to pay to him, as to every other Christian.

But in all other respects our obedience is due to the jurisdiction of the Bishop of Cærleon, who is alone under God our ruler, to keep us right in the way of salvation.

Appendix B

St. Patrick's Breastplate

The 'Breastplate Prayer,' attributed to Saint Patrick, is thought to have been proclaimed whilst Patrick was in spiritual warfare, as he prepared to preach Christ to the hostile pagan King of Ireland. Within this prayer we find his biblical commitment to Christian doctrine and faith that Patrick's God is greater than the pagan gods of Ireland. As an act of proclamation of his faith, Patrick's declaration finds a synthesis with Paul's call to spiritual warfare, and should be understood in this context.

The Armour of God

'Finally, my brethren, be strong in the Lord and in the power of His might. Put on the whole armour of God, that you may be able to stand against the wiles of the devil. For we do not wrestle against flesh and blood, but against principalities, against powers, against the rulers of the darkness of this age, against spiritual hosts of wickedness in the heavenly places. Therefore take up the whole armour of God, that you may be able to withstand in the evil day, and having done all, to stand. Stand therefore, having girded your waist with truth, having put on the breastplate of righteousness, and having shod your feet with the preparation of the gospel of peace; above all, taking the shield of faith with which you will be able to quench all the fiery darts of the wicked one. And take the helmet of salvation, and the sword of the Spirit, which is the word of God; praying always with all prayer and supplication in the Spirit, being watchful to this end with all perseverance and supplication for all the saints' (Ephesians 6:10-18).

St Patrick's Breastplate, with excerpts below, has been transmitted to us from the ninth century *Book of Armagh*.

I bind to myself today,

The strong virtue of the invocation of the Trinity,
I believe in the Trinity in unity,
The Creator of the universe.

I bind to myself today,

The virtue of the incarnation of Christ with His baptism,
The virtue of His crucifixion with His burial,
The virtue of His resurrection with His ascension,
The virtue of His coming on Judgment Day.

I bind to myself today,

The virtue of the love of seraphim,
In the obedience of angels,
In the hope of resurrection unto reward,
In prayers of patriarchs,
In predictions of prophets,
In preaching of apostles,
In faith of confessors,
In purity of holy virgins,
In deeds of righteous men.

I bind to myself today,

God's power to guide me,
God's might to uphold me,
God's wisdom to teach me,
God's eye to watch over me,
God's ear to hear me.

God's word to give me speech,
God's hand to guide me,
God's way to lie before me,
God's shield to shelter me,
God's host to secure me.

Against the snares of demons,
Against the seductions of vices,
Against the lusts of nature,
Against all who meditates injury to me,
Whether far or near,
Whether few or with many.

I invoke today all these virtues,

Against every hostile merciless power,
Which may assail my body and my soul,
Against the incantations of false prophets,
Against the black laws of heathenism,
Against the false laws of heresy,
Against the deceits of idolatry,
Against the spells of women,
And smiths and druids,
Against every knowledge,
That binds the soul of man.

Christ, protect me today,
Against every poison,
Against burning,
Against drowning,
Against death wound,
That I may receive abundant reward.

Christ with me,
Christ before me,
Christ behind me,
Christ within me,
Christ beneath me,
Christ above me,
Christ at my right,
Christ at my left,
Christ when I lie down,
Christ when I rest,
Christ in the quiet,
Christ when I arise.

Christ in the heart of all who thinks of me,
Christ in the mouth of all who speaks to me,
Christ in every eye that sees me,
Christ in every ear that hears me.

I bind to myself today,
The strong virtue of the invocation of the Trinity,
I believe in the Trinity in unity,
The Creator of the universe.

Appendix C

The Nicene Creed

The Nicene Creed was first adopted in AD 325 at the First Council of Nicaea. It was accepted by Celtic Christians and is echoed in their writings and prayers.

We believe in one God,
The Father, the Almighty,
Maker of heaven and earth,
Of all that is, seen and unseen.

We believe in one Lord, Jesus Christ,
The only Son of God,
Eternally begotten of the Father,
God from God, Light from Light,
True God from true God,
Begotten, not made,
Of one Being with the Father.
Through Him all things were made.

For us and for our salvation,
He came down from heaven,
By the power of the Holy Spirit,
He became incarnate,
From the virgin Mary,
And was made Man.

For our sake He was crucified under Pontius Pilate,
He suffered death and was buried,
On the third day He rose again,
In accordance with the Scriptures,
He ascended into heaven,
And is seated at the right hand of the Father.

He will come again in glory,
To judge the living and the dead,
And His Kingdom will have no end.

We believe in the Holy Spirit,
The Lord, the Giver of life,
Who proceeds from the Father and the Son.
With the Father and the Son,
He is worshipped and glorified,
He has spoken through the prophets.

We believe in one holy catholic [Meaning universal],
And apostolic Church.
We acknowledge one baptism,
For the forgiveness of sins.
We look for the resurrection of the dead,
And the life of the world to come.

Amen.

Appendix D

A Prayer of King Alfred

The following prayer from King Alfred the Great can be found chronicled at the end of his translation of *On the Consolation of Philosophy*. In this ninth century prayer, Alfred continues to express Celtic phrases and belief.

Lord God Almighty, Maker and Ruler of all creation, in the name of Thy great mercy...

I beseech Thee, guide me better than I have deserved of Thee; direct me according to Thy will and the needs of my soul better than I myself am able.

Strengthen my mind for Thy will and the needs of my soul. Make me steadfast against the temptations of the devil; keep every foul lust and all evil far from me. Shield me from my enemies, seen and unseen.

Teach me to do Thy holy will, that I may love Thee above all things, with clean thought and chaste body.

For Thou art my Maker and my Redeemer, my life, my comfort, my trust and my hope.

Praise and glory be to Thee now and forever, and unto the endless ages. Amen.

Books by the Author

- *Holy Spirit Power: Knowing the Voice, Guidance and Person of the Holy Spirit*
- *Heaven: A Journey to Paradise and the Heavenly City*
- *The Exodus Evidence In Pictures – The Bible's Exodus:* 100+ colour photos
- *The Ark of the Covenant – Investigating the Ten Leading Claims:* 80+ colour photos
- *Jesus Today, Daily Devotional: 100 Days with Jesus Christ*
- *How Christianity Made the Modern World*
- *Britain, A Christian Country*
- *Celtic Christianity and the First Christian Kings in Britain*
- *The Baptism of Fire, Personal Revival*
- *Glimpses of Glory*
- *Lost Treasures of the Bible*
- *The End Times: A Journey Through the Last Days. The Book of Revelation*
- *Samuel Rees Howells: A Life of Intercession* by Richard Maton, with Paul and Mathew Backholer

Sources and Notes

Chapter One: Celtic Faith
1. Religions, Christianity in Britain, BBC.co.uk/religion, 2 July 2014.
2. Christianity, A History, Dark Ages, by Dr Robert Bedford, Channel 4, 2009.
3. *Adversus Judaeos* by Tertullian, Part 7:4, c.AD 200.
4. *Demonstratio Evangelica* by Eusebius, Book 3, chapter 5, AD 311.
5. Significance of the Lullingstone Roman Villa by English Heritage, english-heritage.org.uk, 4 August 2014.
6. The British state mustn't let go of the Church by Michael Portillo, *Telegraph*, 16 January 2009.
7. The 'Lead Tank' from Icklingham, British Museum, 4 August 2014.
8. Silver plaque and Gold Disc from Water Newton, British Museum, 4 August 2014.
9. Cup from the Water Newton treasure, British Museum, 4 August 2014.
10. *De Synodis or De fide Orientalium* by the Bishop of Poitiers, point 11, AD 358.
11. *Collected Works of John Chrysostom*, Nicene and Post-Nicene Fathers, London, 1889.
12. *De Excidio et Conquestu Britanniae* by Gildas the Wise, AD 540.
13. Historians can find no mention of Joseph of Arimathea until the thirteenth century, in the copy of *Life of Mary Magdalene* attributed to Rabanus Maurus.

Chapter Two: Invasion and Hope
1. How God made the English, a white and Christian people? by Diarmaid MacCulloch, BBC, 31 March 2012.
2. Ibid.
3. Ibid.
4. Ibid.
5. Christianity, A History, Dark Ages by Dr Robert Bedford, Channel 4, 2009.

Chapter Three: Patrick and Ireland
1. *The Confession of St. Patrick,* translated from the Latin by Ludwig Bieler, c.AD 440.
2. Ibid.
3. Ibid.
4. Ibid.
5. Ibid.
6. How the Celts Saved Britain, A New Civilisation, with Dan Snow, BBC, October 2010.
7. Patricius: The True Story of St. Patrick by David Kithcart, CBN.com.
8. *The Confession of St. Patrick,* translated from the Latin by Ludwig Bieler, c.AD 440.
9. Saints and Sinners: Britain's Millennium of Monasteries with Dr Janina Ramirez, BBC, 23 February 2015.
10. *The Confession of St. Patrick,* translated from the Latin by Ludwig Bieler, c.AD 440.
11. Ibid.
12. Christianity, A History, Rome, with Michael Portillo, Channel 4, 2009.
13. The British state mustn't let go of the Church by Michael Portillo,

Telegraph, 16 January 2009.
14. *The Confession of St. Patrick,* translated from the Latin by Ludwig Bieler, c.AD 440.
15. Ibid.

Chapter Four: The Celtic Light in Ireland, Scotland, England and Wales
1. How the Celts Saved Britain, A New Civilisation, with Dan Snow, BBC, October 2010.
2. How the Celts Saved Britain, Salvation, with Dan Snow, BBC, October 2010.
3. Ibid.
4. Christianity, A History, Dark Ages by Dr Robert Bedford, Channel 4, 2009.
5. *Ecclesiastical History of the English People* by Bede, Book III, 731, chapter 2.
6. How the Celts Saved Britain, Salvation, with Dan Snow, BBC, October 2010.
7. Ibid.
8. Ibid.
9. Treasures of the Anglo-Saxons by Dr Janina Ramirez, BBC, 10 August 2010.

Chapter Five: The Celtic Mission to Europe
1. How the Celts Saved Britain, A New Civilisation, with Dan Snow, BBC, October 2010.
2. Ibid.
3. Christianity, A History, Dark Ages, by Dr Robert Bedford, Channel 4, 2009.

Chapter Six: A New Brand of Faith
1. Christianity, A History, Rome, with Michael Portillo, Channel 4, 2009.
2. North Yorkshire, Archaeology, Constantine the Great, by James Gerrard, BBC.co.uk, 27 September 2005.
3. Christianity, A History, Rome, with Michael Portillo, Channel 4, 2009.
4. Ibid.
5. Ibid.
6. Ibid.
7. Ibid.
8. *Codex Theodosianus* XVI 1.2. by Emperor Theodosius I, AD 439.
9. Ibid.
10. Christianity, A History, Rome, with Michael Portillo, Channel 4, 2009.
11. Ibid.
12. Ibid.

Chapter Seven: Supremacy
1. How the Celts Saved Britain, Salvation, with Dan Snow, BBC, October 2010.
2. Silver and gold buckle decorated with a fish from Crundale Down, Kent, Anglo-Saxon, mid-seventh century, British Museum.
3. Treasures of the Anglo-Saxons by Dr Janina Ramirez, BBC, 10 August 2010.
4. Christianity, A History, Dark Ages, with Dr Robert Bedford, Channel 4, 2009.
5. Ibid.
6. Ibid.
7. *Ecclesiastical History of the English Nation*, Book III, by Bede, 731, Chapter XXV.

8. Ibid.

9. Ibid.

10. Ibid.

11. How the Celts Saved Britain, Salvation, with Dan Snow, BBC, October 2010.

12. *An Introduction to Anglo-Saxon England* by Peter Hunter Blair, Cambridge University Press, 1977, p.129.

13. How the Celts Saved Britain, Salvation, with Dan Snow, BBC, October 2010.

14. Treasures of the Anglo-Saxons by Dr Janina Ramirez, BBC, 10 August 2010.

15. The Chapel is assumed to be that of 'Ythanceaster' mentioned by Bede, book III, chapter XXII.

16. Saints and Sinners: Britain's Millennium of Monasteries, with Dr Janina Ramirez, BBC, 23 February 2015.

17. How God made the English, a chosen people? by Diarmaid MacCulloch, BBC, 17 March 2012.

18. Ibid.

19. Christianity, A History, Dark Ages by Dr Robert Bedford, Channel 4, 2009.

20. Ibid.

Chapter Eight: King Alfred and Christianity

1. How God made the English, a chosen people? by Diarmaid MacCulloch, BBC, 17 March 2012.

2. The anonymous account of the *Translation of St Cuthbert*, 1104. Later reprinted in *The Biographical Writings and Letters of Venerable Bede*, translated from the Latin by J. A. Giles; James Bohn, London, 1845, pp.181-218.

3. Ibid.

4. Ibid.

5. *The History of the English Speaking Peoples*, Volume 1, by Winston Churchill, Chapter IV, Henry II, Cassel and co, 1956.

6. Ibid.

7. How God made the English, a chosen people? by Diarmaid MacCulloch, BBC, 17 March 2012.

8. Treasures of the Anglo-Saxons by Dr Janina Ramirez, BBC, 10 August 2010.

9. King Alfred to Bishop Wærferth, preface to *Pastoral Care* by Pope Gregory. The original book dates to AD 590.

10. Ibid.

11. Ibid.

12. Ibid.

13. Christianity, A History, Dark Ages by Dr Robert Bedford, Channel 4, 2009.

14. How God made the English, a chosen people? by Diarmaid MacCulloch, BBC, 17 March 2012.

ByFaith Media Books

Revival Fires and Awakenings – Thirty-Six Visitations of the Holy Spirit by Mathew Backholer.

Reformation to Revival, 500 Years of God's Glory: Sixty Revivals, Awakenings and Heaven-Sent Visitations of the Holy Spirit by Mathew Backholer

How to Plan, Prepare and Successfully Complete Your Short-Term Mission by Mathew Backholer.

Revival Fire – 150 Years of Revivals by Mathew Backholer documents twelve revivals from ten countries.

Discipleship for Everyday Living by Mathew Backholer. A dynamic biblical book for Christian growth.

Global Revival, Worldwide Outpourings, Forty-Three Visitations of the Holy Spirit by Mathew Backholer.

Understanding Revival and Addressing the Issues it Provokes by Mathew Backholer.

Extreme Faith – On Fire Christianity by Mathew Backholer. Powerful foundations for faith in Christ!

Revival Answers: True and False Revivals by Mathew Backholer. What is genuine and false revival?

Short-Term Missions, A Christian Guide to STMs, For Leaders, Pastors, Students... by Mathew Backholer.

Budget Travel, A Guide to Travelling on a Shoestring Explore the World, A Discount Overseas Adventure Trip: Gap Year, Backpacking by Mathew Backholer

Prophecy Now, Prophetic Words and Divine Revelations, For You, the Church and the Nations by Michael Backholer.

Samuel Rees Howells: A Life of Intercession by Richard Maton. Learn how intercession and prayer changed history.

Samuel, Son and Successor of Rees Howells by Richard Maton. Discover the full biography of Samuel Rees Howells.

The Holy Spirit in a Man by R.B. Watchman. An autobiography.

Tares and Weeds in your Church: Trouble & Deception in God's House by R.B. Watchman.

How Christianity Made the Modern World by Paul Backholer.

Holy Spirit Power: Knowing the Voice, Guidance and Person of the Holy Spirit by Paul Backholer.

Heaven: A Journey to Paradise and the Heavenly City by Paul Backholer.

The Exodus Evidence In Pictures – The Bible's Exodus by Paul Backholer. 100+ colour photos.

The Ark of the Covenant – Investigating the Ten Leading Claims by Paul Backholer. 80+ colour photos.

Jesus Today, Daily Devotional: 100 Days with Jesus Christ by Paul Backholer.

Britain, A Christian Country by Paul Backholer.

Celtic Christianity and the First Christian Kings in Britain by Paul Backholer.

The Baptism of Fire, Personal Revival and the Anointing for Supernatural Living by Paul Backholer.

Glimpses of Glory, Revelations in the Realms of God by Paul Backholer

Lost Treasures of the Bible by Paul Backholer.

The End Times: A Journey Through the Last Days. The Book of Revelation...by Paul Backholer.

Debt Time Bomb! Debt Mountains: The Financial Crisis and its Toxic Legacy by Paul Backholer. Ebook.

www.ByFaithBooks.co.uk

ByFaith Media DVDs

Great Christian Revivals on 1 DVD is an uplifting account of some of the greatest revivals in Church history. Filmed on location across Britain and drawing upon archive information, the stories of the Welsh Revival (1904-1905), the Hebridean Revival (1949-1952) and the Evangelical Revival (1739-1791), are told in this 72 minute documentary.

ByFaith – Quest for the Ark of the Covenant on 1 DVD. Experience an adventure and investigate the mystery of the lost Ark of the Covenant! Explore Ethiopia's rock churches; find the Egyptian Pharaoh who entered Solomon's Temple and search for the Queen of Sheba's Palace. Four episodes. 100+ minutes.

ByFaith – World Mission on 1 DVD. Pack your backpack and join two adventurers as they travel through 14 nations on their global short-term mission (STM). Get inspired for your STM, as you watch this 85 minute adventure; filmed over three years.

Israel in Egypt – The Exodus Mystery on 1 DVD. A four year quest searching for the evidence for Joseph, Moses and the Hebrew Slaves in Egypt. Explore the Exodus route, hunt for the Red Sea and climb Mount Sinai. This is the best of the eight episode TV series *ByFaith – In Search of the Exodus.* 110+ minutes.

ByFaith – In Search of the Exodus on 2 DVDs. The quest to find the evidence for ancient Israel in Egypt, the Red Sea and Sinai, in eight episodes. 200+ minutes.

Visit **www.ByFaith.org** to watch the trailers for these DVDs and for more information.
www.ByFaithDVDs.co.uk

Notes

Notes

Notes

Notes

Notes

Lightning Source UK Ltd.
Milton Keynes UK
UKHW020731190221
378997UK00013B/775